149

W9-BUY-219

WELCOME TO COLONIAL WILLIAMSBURG

A visit to Colonial Williamsburg is a rendezvous with one of the most important chapters of America's history and with an entire community that existed more than two centuries ago. The experience includes encounters with the great deeds of patriot leaders as well as with the daily activities of the less well-known people who also lived in eighteenth-century Williamsburg and whose contributions to the ideals and values expressed here were equally significant. The result is a new awareness of and kinship with the men, women, and children of early America. Much of the thinking and action that led to the creation of our nation took place in eighteenth-century Williamsburg. For example, the Virginia Declaration of Rights, written by George Mason, was the basis for the Bill of Rights—the first ten amendments to the U. S. Constitution.

People from all walks of life created the Virginia colony, and here in Williamsburg visitors see public buildings, trade shops, stores, town houses, and homes of the "middling sort." Gentry, planters, merchants, indentured servants, free blacks, slaves, travelers, and foreign visitors all congregated in the colony's capital.

Buildings, gardens, and other physical reminders of the past are only part of a visit to Colonial Williamsburg. The programs in the Historic Area re-create a living, changing town where people worked, dined, shopped, and visited. Modern visitors discover the cares, accomplishments, and failures of residents in and travelers to Virginia's colonial capital. Colonial Williamsburg strives to provide an experience that is enjoyable, educational, and relevant to life today.

"That the future may learn from the past." This is the mission of Colonial Williamsburg. We strive to help our visitors, and those we reach beyond this city, to draw understanding, wisdom, and inspiration from the lessons of history. Thomas Jefferson believed that an educated citizenry is the best defense of democratic freedoms. Colonial Williamsburg honors and represents, as it has for more than 75 years, the ideals, values, and hopes on which America was founded.

Your patronage is the single largest source of support for Colonial Williamsburg's museum and educational programs. The balance of the annual cost of preserving and maintaining the Historic Area and of presenting those programs is funded by donors' generous contributions, sales of craft objects, reproductions, and educational materials, revenues from hotel and restaurant operations, rental property income, and endowment income.

All of us at Colonial Williamsburg appreciate the many ways in which you support our programs and purposes. Your participation is essential to the long-term future of this special place.

Colin G. Campbell, *Chairman and President*
The Colonial Williamsburg Foundation

OFFICIAL GUIDE TO
COLONIAL WILLIAMSBURG

NEW EDITION

Text by Michael Olmert

New Text by Suzanne E. Coffman

Drawings of Buildings by Peter C. Turner

Maps by Louis Luedtke

Design by Helen Mageras Olds and Richard Stinely

Photography by Dave M. Doody, Tom Green, Hans Lorenz, and
additional staff photographers

The Colonial Williamsburg Foundation

Williamsburg, Virginia

© 1998 by
The Colonial Williamsburg Foundation

Fourth printing, 2002

All rights reserved, including the right to reproduce this book or
portions thereof in any form

Library of Congress Cataloging-in-Publication Data

Olmert, Michael.
    Official guide to Colonial Williamsburg / text by
Michael Olmert ; new text by Suzanne E. Coffman ;
drawings of buildings by Peter C. Turner ; maps by
Louis Luedtke. — New ed.
        p.   cm.
    Includes bibliographical references (p.   ) and index.
    ISBN 0-87935-184-5 (pbk.)
        1. Williamsburg (Va.)—Guidebooks. I. Coffman,
Suzanne E., 1958– . II. Colonial Williamsburg Foundation.
III. Title.
F234.W7046 1998
917.55'42520441—dc21   98-17476
                                                             CIP

Photographs taken in Colonial Williamsburg by visitors must
be intended for their personal use only. Such photographs may not
be used for commercial purposes.

Printed in the United States of America

*The Frenchman's Map on page 16 is reproduced courtesy of
Earl Gregg Swem Library, the College of William and Mary,
Williamsburg, Virginia.*

The detail from the portrait of Peyton Randolph *on page
107 is reproduced courtesy of the Virginia Historical Society,
Richmond, Virginia.*

CONTENTS

YOUR VISIT TO COLONIAL WILLIAMSBURG

*D*ebate revolutionary ideas with Thomas Jefferson, Patrick Henry, or George Washington. See prominent colonial citizens wearing the fashions of the eighteenth century. Encounter the African-American slaves and free blacks who made the Virginia colony's prosperity possible. Watch tradespeople work in their shops. Dine in a colonial tavern on fare based on early American recipes. Experience what it was like to live in the capital of Virginia on the eve of the American Revolution.

A visit to Colonial Williamsburg is a journey into America's past. Here, in the restored capital of eighteenth-century Virginia and at neighboring Carter's Grove, you will enter the world of people who lived more than two hundred years ago. By making decisions that defined the course of our nation's history, they shaped the world we inhabit today.

Colonial Williamsburg is also one of the country's premier destination resorts. Excellent dining establishments, shopping, hotels, and award-winning golf courses are all within walking distance of Colonial Williamsburg's Historic Area. Just southwest is Jamestown, where English colonization took root in 1607 and the friendship of Captain John Smith and Pocahontas grew. Just southeast is Yorktown, where George Washington and the Continental army defeated the British 174 years later. Drive about an hour southeast of Williamsburg to enjoy Virginia's beaches; drive the same distance northwest to explore the state capital and the Civil War battlefields around Richmond.

Welcome to Colonial Williamsburg.

CHECKLIST: WHAT IS COLONIAL WILLIAMSBURG?

A place where you can:

- [ ] *Travel back in time to the era when Thomas Jefferson, Patrick Henry, and George Washington helped spark the American Revolution*

- [ ] *Meet the patriot leaders, tradespeople, shopkeepers, laborers, and free and enslaved African-Americans who created a new nation*

- [ ] *Take in fascinating museum exhibitions, special lectures, and tours*

- [ ] *Dine in colonial taverns and twenty-first-century restaurants*

- [ ] *Stay in world-class hotels, tee up on award-winning golf courses, and enjoy other resort amenities just steps from the eighteenth century*

- [ ] *Find authentic Colonial Williamsburg merchandise in any of our twenty-eight stores inside and adjacent to the Historic Area*

WHAT IS COLONIAL WILLIAMSBURG?
A TRIP TO A DIFFERENT PLACE AND TIME. AMERICA'S BIRTHPLACE.
A CHANCE TO GET REACQUAINTED WITH YOUR COUNTRY.

BEFORE YOU VISIT COLONIAL WILLIAMSBURG

Before you make your reservations, consider what you want to do while you're here. Review this guide to see what interests you and your family the most. For your convenience, you can now reserve hotel rooms, admission tickets, and vacation packages on-line.

Internet. If you have access to the Internet, visit http://www.colonialwilliamsburg.com. Our Web site has a wealth of information about the Historic Area, evening and special programs, museums, tickets, our hotels, and our restaurants.

Vacation Planner. The Vacation Planner offers a general overview of Colonial Williamsburg programs and facilities. It also contains information on the different types of admission tickets, year-round and special events, and package plans at the hotels. Call 1-800-HISTORY or e-mail us at cwres@cwf.org to request a copy of the Vacation Planner.

CHECKLIST: PLANNING YOUR VISIT

For information or to make reservations for tickets, package plans at Colonial Williamsburg's hotels, and programs and activities during your visit:

☐ *Call 1-800-HISTORY or*
☐ *If you have access to the Internet, visit ColonialWilliamsburg's Web site at http://www.colonialwilliamsburg.com*

Phone-in Reservations. You can also make lodging and dining reservations and to purchase your admission and evening program tickets, by calling 1-800-HISTORY. Our guest services agents can help you select programs that will appeal to you and your family.

Why You Want to Buy a Ticket. Your admission ticket is your passport to the programs and sites in the Historic Area, our ninety acres of gardens and greens, and our world-class museums.

Talk with the patriot printer of the *Virginia Gazette*. Learn what a middle-class housewife thinks will happen to her husband and children if war comes. Find out what "all men are created equal" means to an African-American slave. Watch master tradespeople use eighteenth-century techniques to create exquisite silver bowls, utilitarian ironwares, fashionable gowns, and functional baskets. Stand in the House of Burgesses, where Patrick Henry railed against the Stamp Act. Admire the majesty of the Governor's Palace, then learn how the "middling sort" lived at the James Geddy or Benjamin Powell House. Stroll by elegant boxwood topiaries and through informal kitchen gardens.

Continue exploring the past at our museums. See the elegant and everyday objects colonial Virginians lived with at the DeWitt Wallace Decorative Arts Museum. Admire the nation's premier collection of American folk art at the Abby Aldrich Rockefeller Folk Art Museum. Explore four hundred years of history at Carter's Grove. Visit the

Winthrop Rockefeller Archaeology Museum to learn how archaeology rediscovered a seventeenth-century settlement previously lost to history.

Your admission ticket does more than give you access to buildings. It opens the door to a different era.

Visitors with Special Needs. Colonial Williamsburg wants all visitors to enjoy their experience here. If you have special needs, call 757-220-7645 (voice) or 757-565-8938 (TTY) about four weeks before your visit to:

☐ Request copies of *A Guide for Visitors with Disabilities* and *Wheelchair Users Guide to Colonial Williamsburg*. Information is also available on-line at https://www.colonialwilliamsburg.com/visit/see_do/handicap.html

☐ Schedule signing interpreters or guides for the visually impaired

CHECKLIST: WHAT TO PACK

☐ *Comfortable shoes. You'll be walking to buildings, around them, and through them. Walking at a comfortable pace, you can go from the east to the west end of the Historic Area (about a mile) in approximately twenty minutes.*

☐ *Appropriate clothes for the weather. Summers are hot and humid. Spring and fall days can change quickly from temperate to warm or cold. The usually mild winters can be punctuated by days in the single digits. Check the long-range forecast before you visit.*

☐ *Coat and tie if you will be having dinner or Sunday brunch in the Regency Room at the Williamsburg Inn. Casual dress is appropriate everywhere else at Colonial Williamsburg.*

Your admission ticket is your passport to the sites and programs in the Historic Area.

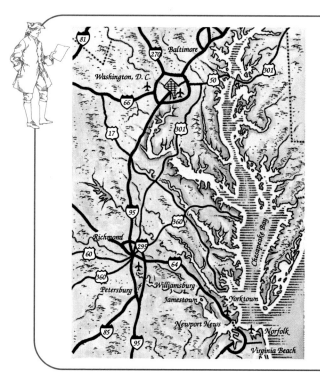

CHECKLIST: HOW TO GET TO COLONIAL WILLIAMSBURG

BY CAR. *Colonial Williamsburg is located 150 miles south of Washington, D. C., midway between Richmond and Norfolk. Take Interstate 64 to exit 238. After exiting, look for the green and white signs for the Visitor Center.*

BY AIR. *Newport News–Williamsburg International Airport is twenty minutes from Colonial Williamsburg; Richmond International Airport and Norfolk International Airport are both fifty minutes away. Each airport has rental car and limousine services.*

BY TRAIN OR BUS. *Amtrak serves the Williamsburg Transportation Center with a connecting train from Washington, D. C. The Center is just blocks from the Historic Area and provides car rentals, a cab stand, and Greyhound bus connections.*

☐ Braille guides to the Historic Area may be borrowed from the Colonial Williamsburg Visitor Center

☐ Get information on wheelchair rentals, portable wheelchair ramps, special parking passes, parking in the Historic Area and at Carter's Grove, Colonial Williamsburg buses equipped with wheelchair lifts, and other services

Because of limited accessibility at some sites, visitors with disabilities receive a discount on admission tickets. The Visitor Center, hotels, and twenty-first-century restaurants, shops, and museums are largely accessible.

Foreign Visitors. At the Visitor Center, foreign visitors can listen to the appropriate foreign language tape while viewing the film *Williamsburg—The Story of a Patriot.*

How Long to Visit. Plan to stay several days, because it's next to impossible to do everything in a single day. Make your reservations as early as possible, especially for Easter, Thanksgiving, and the Christmas season.

Then travel across the miles to Colonial Williamsburg, where you'll travel back in time to the eve of the American Revolution.

AFTER YOU ARRIVE AT COLONIAL WILLIAMSBURG

At the Visitor Center. You can buy your tickets at several locations in Colonial Williamsburg and at many local hotels and motels, but all visitors should begin their trip into the past at the Visitor Center. If you have not already purchased your tickets and made lodging, dining, and evening program reservations, the Visitor Center staff can help you plan your visit, select the appropriate ticket options, and make reservations for dining, lodging, and special programs. You may also want to stop by the

CHECKLIST: AT THE VISITOR CENTER

☐ *Purchase your admission and evening program tickets, if you have not already done so*

☐ *See* Williamsburg—The Story of a Patriot

☐ *Get a* Visitor's Companion

☐ *Ask about the Orientation Walk*

☐ *Make reservations for Walking Tours*

☐ *Purchase carriage or wagon ride tickets*

☐ *Exchange twenty-first-century dollars for Colonial Currency*

☐ *Make dining and lodging reservations, if you have not already done so*

☐ *Browse for books or grab a cup of coffee at Williamsburg Booksellers; pick up a special souvenir T-shirt or other memento at Williamsburg Marketplace*

☐ *Take the bus to the Historic Area*

Learning Resource Center (inside Williamsburg Booksellers) at the Visitor Center to learn about programs that appeal to children. (See the Educational Services and Outreach section in this guide for more information on the Learning Resource Center.) With your ticket you will receive a copy of the *Visitor's Companion,* which lists the programs being offered in the Historic Area and the museums. Be sure to see *Williamsburg—The Story of a Patriot.* This dramatization of events in Williamsburg on the eve of the American Revolution plays throughout the day at the Visitor Center and in most area hotel and motel rooms.

Other Ticket Sales Locations. Tickets and information are also available at the Gateway Building, Lumber House ticket office, and Tickets, Treasures and Books in the Historic Area; Merchants Square Ticket Office adjacent to the Historic Area; and Colonial Williamsburg's hotels. Several Williamsburg-area hotels and motels also offer Colonial Williamsburg admission tickets, although they do not have evening or special program tickets.

Orientation Walk, Walking Tours, Carriage and Wagon Rides. All visitors are encouraged to take the thirty-minute Orientation Walk. You'll get a quick overview of the town and the things you can see and do in the Historic Area. Ask about the Orientation Walk at any ticket sales location. Sixty-minute Walking Tours, offered mid-March through December, explore topics such as the American Revolution, African-American life in colonial Virginia, religion in the colony, and consumerism during the eighteenth century. Make reservations for Walking Tours at any ticket sales location on the day of the walk. Tickets for carriage or wagon rides can be purchased at any ticket sales location on the day of the ride. Rides sell out quickly during peak seasons, so buy your tickets early in the day.

Colonial Currency. You may exchange modern money for replicas of colonial currency that can be used for any purchase in the Historic Area. Exchange your twenty-first-century dollars for Colonial Currency at the Visitor Center, or any ticket sales location. Visitors of all ages will have fun using the money and learning about the economy of eighteenth-century Virginia.

Colonial Williamsburg Buses, Walking Path to the Historic Area. As you leave the Visitor Center, you will find buses waiting to take you directly to the Historic Area. All guests of Colonial Williamsburg's hotels and all visitors who have purchased admission tickets may ride our shuttle buses. Streets in the Historic Area are closed to motor vehicles, and there is no regular visitor parking there. If you are staying at a Colonial Williamsburg hotel, leave your car at your hotel and walk to the Historic Area. If you are staying somewhere else, leave your car at the Visitor Center and take the bus from there. You may also walk to the Historic Area along a wooded path that goes from the Visitor Center to the Gateway Building in the Historic Area.

CHECKLIST: BUYING YOUR TICKETS

The most convenient way to purchase Colonial Williamsburg tickets is by calling 1-800-HISTORY before you visit. Once you are here, you can buy your tickets at the:

☐ *Visitor Center*

☐ *Gateway Building (in the Historic Area)*

☐ *Lumber House ticket office (in the Historic Area)*

☐ *Tickets, Treasures and Books (in the Historic Area)*

☐ *Merchants Square Ticket Office (adjacent to the Historic Area)*

Guests of Colonial Williamsburg's hotels can purchase their tickets at the:

☐ *Williamsburg Inn*

☐ *Williamsburg Lodge*

☐ *Governor's Inn*

☐ *Colonial Houses*

☐ *Providence Hall (see the concierge or front desk at the Inn)*

☐ *Providence Hall House (see the concierge or front desk at the Inn)*

Several Williamsburg-area hotels and motels also carry Colonial Williamsburg admission tickets. They do not have tickets for evening programs and other special events, however.

YOU ARE READY TO VISIT THE EIGHTEENTH CENTURY.

SIGNIFICANT MOMENTS IN WILLIAMSBURG'S HISTORY

1607   First permanent English settlement in North America established at Jamestown.

1693   College of William and Mary founded.

1699   Virginia's capital moved from Jamestown to Williamsburg.

1765   May 30. Patrick Henry delivers his ringing "Caesar–Brutus" speech in opposition to the Stamp Act.

1769   Virginia protests new British taxes and boycotts British goods.

1774   **June 1.** Williamsburg citizens observe a day of fasting, humiliation, and prayer to protest Parliament's closing of the port of Boston.

   August. Virginia's leaders elect delegates to the first Continental Congress in Philadelphia.

1775   **April 21.** Governor Dunmore has the colony's powder removed from the Magazine. Only the efforts of Williamsburg's moderate leaders prevent an angry mob from marching on the Governor's Palace.

   June 8. The royal governor and his family flee the Palace.

1776   **May 15.** Virginia's legislators instruct their delegates in Philadelphia to propose independence, leading directly to the adoption of the Declaration of Independence on July 4.

   June 12. Virginia adopts America's first Declaration of Rights, later the basis for the Bill of Rights of the U. S. Constitution.

   July 6. Patrick Henry inaugurated first governor of the state of Virginia.

1780   Capital moved from Williamsburg to Richmond.

1781   **June 25–July 4.** British occupy Williamsburg.

   September 14. Washington and Rochambeau arrive in Williamsburg to plan campaign against British at Yorktown.

   October 19. British surrender at Yorktown, effectively ending the Revolution.

1862   May 5. Battle of Williamsburg. Union forces occupy Williamsburg for the rest of the Civil War.

1926   John D. Rockefeller, Jr., decides to restore Williamsburg to its eighteenth-century appearance.

1934   President Franklin D. Roosevelt commemorates the restoration, referring to Duke of Gloucester Street as "the most historic avenue in America."

1999   The city of Williamsburg celebrates its three hundredth anniversary.

THE CITY OF WILLIAMSBURG

"WILLIAMSBURG . . . is regularly laid out in parallel streets, intersected by others at right angles; has a handsome square in the center, through which runs the principal street, one of the most spacious in North-America, three quarters of a mile in length, and above a hundred feet wide. At the ends of this street are two public buildings, the college and the capitol: and although the houses are of wood, covered with shingles, and but indifferently built, the whole makes a handsome appearance."

—The Reverend Andrew Burnaby, who came to Virginia from England in 1759 and remained until 1760, described Williamsburg in his *Travels through the Middle Settlements in North-America, in the Years 1759 and 1760*

JAMESTOWN, THE SEVENTEENTH-CENTURY CAPITAL

The story of Williamsburg, the capital of eighteenth-century Virginia, really began at seventeenth-century Jamestown. For over ninety years after the first English adventurers set foot on Virginia soil, Jamestown served as the seat of government and administrative center of England's largest colony in North America. From its statehouse on the banks of the James River, officials and lawmakers governed the colonists, promoted the spread of settlement, and, tragically for the future, sanctioned the importation of African slaves to meet the colony's labor shortage. As Virginia grew, Jamestown did too, but by fits and starts.

When the statehouse burned for the fourth time in 1698, many Virginians, including the royal governor, Francis Nicholson, seized on the accident as an opportunity to move the capital. Several prospective sites were considered. After some debate, members of the House of Burgesses chose a propitious site between the York and James Rivers five miles from the old capital city, an up-and-coming place known as Middle Plantation.

Middle Plantation had been founded in the early seventeenth century as an outpost to defend against Indian attacks. By 1690, it had developed into a prosperous neighborhood of widely scattered houses belonging to successful tobacco planters and merchants. It also contained a church, several stores, a tavern, two mills, and, after 1695, the College of William and Mary. On several occasions, most notably during Bacon's Rebellion in 1676 and 1677, when Jamestown was burned to the ground, Middle Plantation served as a substitute capital. Its main attractions as a potential site for the capital were several. First, it was located on high ground between two rivers and therefore was relatively healthy. Its inland location was thought to be safe from naval bombardment, and it was already the home of the college, one of Virginia's principal institutions. Finally, and perhaps most importantly, several of Virginia's leading politicians lived at Middle Plantation. Begun in 1699, the new city was named Williamsburg in honor of the king of England, William III.

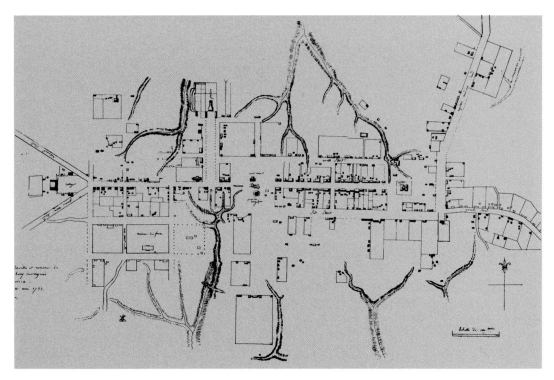

The Frenchman's Map, probably drawn by a French officer for the purpose of billeting troops after the Siege of Yorktown in 1781, shows the streets and many of the buildings of eighteenth-century Williamsburg.

WILLIAMSBURG'S TOWN PLAN AND LANDMARKS

Once the decision was made to move the capital from Jamestown to Middle Plantation, an entirely new capital city was laid out on the site. The desire to design a completely new city fulfilled one of the reasons for moving the capital from Jamestown. Many Virginians thought their colony was becoming too important to be served by anything less than a capital city built to reflect Virginia's preeminence among England's American colonies. In all probability, Governor Nicholson took the initiative for the new design. He had successfully planned Annapolis as governor of Maryland, and he was well versed in the latest principles of urban planning. The town plan of Williamsburg reflected those principles. The fact that it was newly built can be your key to discovering in restored Williamsburg traces of

the eighteenth-century city. Several important physical landmarks were central to Nicholson's plan and are still extant.

The first is a large, open area in the center of the town known as Market Square. Today you will find the Magazine, built on Governor Alexander Spotswood's orders in 1715, and the Courthouse on Market Square. In the eighteenth century, the square served as a town common where markets and fairs were held regularly. Another distinctive feature of the colonial capital that is still present today crosses the square in an east-west direction. Duke of Gloucester Street, or "the Main Street," as it was known in the eighteenth century, extends "uptown" from the College of William and Mary at the western end and "downtown" to the Capitol building at the eastern. Designed to be ninety-nine feet wide and nearly one mile long, this street was a broad, open avenue that highlighted the linear aspects of the city plan.

To the west of Market Square, the city was laid out in the shape of a square centered on Bruton Parish Church. The first church building, completed by 1683, stood a little to the north of the present structure, which replaced it in 1715. Farther to the west is the main college building, called the Wren Building in honor of Sir Christopher Wren, an important seventeenth-century English architect who was reputed (mistakenly) to have inspired its design. Located just outside the eighteenth-century city boundary, the college building was the key visual element at the west end of Duke of Gloucester Street. The symbolic importance of this part of Williamsburg with its religious and educational institutions was and still is reinforced by the Governor's Palace. By its location at the head of a wide, green avenue running north from the church, this landmark was meant to command an eighteenth-century visitor's attention, as it still does that of modern visitors.

If you walk east from Market Square, you will be drawn to the dominant landmark designed for that end of town—the Capitol. To help focus attention on this most important building, the eastern end of Williamsburg was framed by two back streets, Nicholson on the north and Francis on the south.

THE NEW TOWNS OF THE EIGHTEENTH CENTURY

People's early expectations for Williamsburg were inspired by an older vision of what cities could accomplish. Traditionally they were viewed as centers of learning, religion, and government. As you walk along Williamsburg's main street, you can see that the city planners anchored the town on the college, church, and Capitol, the physical symbols of a traditional city. An eighteenth-century visitor to Williamsburg, when it was still little more than a grid of vacant lots, would

have known from these three official buildings that he was in a capital city. But even as Williamsburg began to grow, this older understanding of what a city was meant to be was being supplanted by a newer vision.

In England, in her overseas colonies, and throughout western Europe, people who once were content to acquire relatively few material possessions began to demand more—more clothes, more crockery, more furniture, more books. This surge in consumer demand transformed villages and towns into something that not even great metropolitan cities such as London had been before. Some grew into manufacturing centers, making the goods that consumers increasingly began to demand. Others became retail centers selling affordable goods to regional markets of ordinary buyers.

The effect of this shift toward commerce-centered urban activities was even felt in far-off Virginia. By the mid-eighteenth century, Williamsburg had taken on a more modern look. Retail stores lined the streets, their display windows filled with merchandise priced to suit almost every man's and woman's pocketbook. Artisans like silversmiths and blacksmiths frequently sold imported goods in their shops. Amid the business of government,

The "Bodleian Plate," an engraved copperplate of about 1740, was discovered at Oxford University. Renderings of the Capitol and the Governor's Palace assisted in the reconstruction of those buildings.

Williamsburg catered to a growing number of eager new consumers. Because there is much that you will recognize of our own world here, restored Williamsburg is a bridge to that time when the consumer age was just beginning.

THE WILLIAMSBURG COMMUNITY

Unlike Jamestown, Williamsburg did not remain a small, undeveloped administrative center. Partly because the colony's growth continued throughout the eighteenth century and partly because economic forces reshaped Virginia society, Williamsburg fulfilled the expectation of its founders and kept pace with the growing colony.

At first the business of government attracted the nucleus of Williamsburg's urban population. Joining the small staff already living at the college were the governor, his household, and the clerks of various government offices. Soon the regular meetings of the General Court, the attendance of councillors on the governor, and the periodic meetings of the General Assembly brought a number of other people to Williamsburg to support these governmental activities. Taverns were established to feed and house those in town on government business. Lawyers settled here to be close

to the General Court. As the century progressed, more and more stores were opened to provide merchandise to residents and out-of-town shoppers. The townspeople engaged in these activities needed to be housed and provided with foodstuffs that they didn't grow themselves. Carpenters and masons moved to town to build houses and shops. Bakers, tailors, and barbers settled here to serve both visitors and townspeople. Much of the heavy and domestic work around town was performed by blacks, most of them slaves, although a few were free. By the eve of the American Revolution nearly two thousand men, women, and children—roughly half white, half black—lived in the capital city.

Together these men and women formed a complex community that left traces that you can still see if you pay close attention. As you walk toward the Capitol from Market Square, for example, the increasing density of artisans' shops, stores, taverns, and houses crowding in on the Capitol gives the correct impression that this was the busiest section of town. The townspeople who lived and worked here competed for the business of visitors to the Capitol. A different landscape can be seen around the Courthouse. As you look north and south,

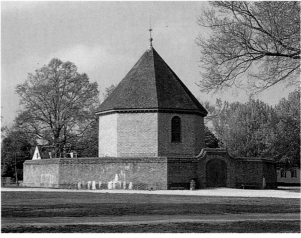

The Magazine was erected in 1715. After the Revolution, it saw use as a market, a Baptist meetinghouse, a dancing school, and a livery stable.

The Prentis Store is Williamsburg's best surviving example of a colonial store. Built in 1739–1740, it survived into the twentieth century as a gas station.

several large town houses meet the eye, as they would have in the late eighteenth century. The clamor of marketplace vendors notwithstanding, the open space of Market Square had a special appeal for the prominent men who built these imposing dwellings. It provided an attractive setting for their homes. After mid-century, the long, open avenue in front of the Governor's Palace offered a similar attraction. Earlier it had faced a jumble of small houses, noisy, dirty workshops, and a theater. Even after the large houses came to be built, the working character of the Palace green lingered here and there.

As you walk past Bruton Parish Church toward the college, you can still glimpse several small, open fields that gave something of a pastoral air to the west end of Williamsburg in the eighteenth century. A few stores, artisans' shops, and taverns line the streets here, but from a businessman's point of view this end of town was not as desirable as downtown near the Capitol. It was common for townspeople living here to buy half-acre lots in blocks of two or more, which they turned into small urban estates. Kitchen and flower gardens filled much of the open space and re-

inforced the residential character that Nicholson intended for this part of the capital. The back streets of Williamsburg—Prince George, Scotland, Ireland, and especially Francis and Nicholson Streets as they extended to the east—strengthened this countrified aspect of the town. Ordinary trade shops commonly adjoined or faced large urban estates along the north and south edges of Williamsburg. In the eighteenth century, the distinction between town and country was blurred and sometimes unsightly. People living along these streets often commented on the pleasant location of their homes, oblivious to the squalor of neighboring slaves and poor whites.

Eighteenth-century travelers to Williamsburg would have experienced some of the same sensations that the restored city offers modern visitors, and others that were utterly different. They would have encountered the hustle and bustle of shops, taverns, and stores. They would have savored pleasing vistas and hurried past byways. They would have heard the sounds of people working, the ringing of bells at the college, church, and Capitol, and the rattle of carriages and wagons moving along the streets. On the way out of town travelers might have held their noses when passing the bodies of criminals left on the gibbet or stood aside to allow passage of a string of slaves in chains on the road from Yorktown to the auction block in the busy capital. Williamsburg in the eighteenth century was a wide-open American town—alive and vibrant—on the edge of empire. You are invited to conjure up colonial Williamsburg in your imagination as you tour the city today.

The restored buildings, antique furnishings, and costumed interpreters can help you re-create a picture of the past in your mind's eye. The townspeople themselves are always the hardest to envision and understand. There are clues everywhere. Look for evidence of London fashions and listen for British and Scottish accents. Colonial towns and cities attracted concentrations of immigrants not to be found in the countryside. Newcomers with skills in the fashion trades found ready employment in commercial centers such as Williamsburg. Town dwellers were eager to engage the services of foreign-trained tutors, dancing masters, doctors, and clerks.

The capital city was seldom the final destination for slaves fresh off the boat from Africa or the West Indies. Usually they were sold directly to planters who broke them in by working them as field hands. Williamsburg's sizable black population was disproportionately native born in contrast to its many newly arrived white inhabitants. Only blacks long settled in the colony had time to acquire the special skills that townspeople valued. Those African-Virginians who lived and worked in Williamsburg had often learned semiskilled trades, could read, cipher, and sometimes write, usually spoke English, and generally were familiar with the ways of white people, however much they kept their own customs among themselves. Interpreters at Colonial Williamsburg can show you all aspects of the urban slave's experience.

Native Americans were seen on these streets, too. Local Indian groups had long since been reduced in number and confined to settlements on land that nobody else wanted. But now and then, local Indians found their way into town. Archaeologists excavate pottery that suggests Native Americans made and traded earthenware bowls and pots used in kitchens and quarters. Occasionally, ambassadors from the Cherokee, Nottoway, and Catawba nations led delegations to the colonial capital to treat with British officials.

Williamsburg was a place to which many

The John Crump House before and after reconstruction.

VIRGINIA'S FAMOUS SIGNERS

". . . we mutually pledge to each other our Lives, our Fortunes, and our sacred Honor."

George Wythe
Richard Henry Lee

Th Jefferson

Benj Harrison
Th Nelson jr.
Francis Lightfoot Lee
Carter Braxton

In the crucial decade before the American Revolution, Williamsburg was a training ground for a remarkable body of men. When it became clear that war with Great Britain could not be avoided, George Wythe, Richard Henry Lee, Thomas Jefferson, Benjamin Harrison, Thomas Nelson, Francis Lightfoot Lee, and Carter Braxton met in Philadelphia with representatives from the other colonies to declare independence from the mother country. On July 4, 1776, the Continental Congress formally adopted the Declaration of Independence and took the first momentous step toward establishing a new nation.

G Washington

George Washington did not sign the Declaration of Independence because in July 1776 he was in New York preparing to defend Manhattan against the British.

came seeking their fortunes, however meager they may have been for slaves, Indians, and immigrants with few skills. The town was a crucible where people from different backgrounds shaped and were shaped by their encounters with one another. The ceaseless tug-of-war among the diverse peoples who met in North America and settled in towns like Williamsburg receives special attention from interpreters at Colonial Williamsburg today because those encounters forged our American values and eventually our very identity. The struggle to be both free and equal has been a dynamic force in our democracy for more than two hundred years. At Colonial Williamsburg it is the central theme in the history lesson we call "Becoming Americans."

WILLIAMSBURG AFTER THE WAR

For eighty years, Williamsburg was Virginia's capital. Although it grew into a far more impressive urban community than had Jamestown, not all eighteenth-century Virginians were happy that the capital was located here. Several times, Williamsburg supporters had to beat back efforts to move the capital someplace else. But in 1780, for reasons similar to those offered in 1699—military defense, healthier climate, and a more central location—proponents of a new capital prevailed. The capital of Revolutionary Virginia removed to Richmond, where it remains today.

Despite the loss of the capital, Williamsburg did not die as Jamestown had. It continued to be a county seat, and it continued to house

Dr. W. A. R. Goodwin (left), *who dreamed of restoring eighteenth-century Williamsburg, and John D. Rockefeller, Jr., who made the dream a reality*

two important institutions—the College of William and Mary and the Public Hospital for the insane. Throughout the nineteenth century, Williamsburg served as a major market center for nearby farmers and their families. As a quiet college and market town, it witnessed the Civil War firsthand, experienced the emancipation of slaves, and welcomed the railroad in the 1880s. Although fires occasionally raged in parts of the old city, Williamsburg was spared major destruction. Old eighteenth-century homes were repaired, renovated, and continued in use until the twentieth century.

Then, in the early years of the twentieth century, the Reverend W. A. R. Goodwin, rector of Bruton Parish, had a visionary idea. Inspired by the surviving eighteenth-century character of Williamsburg and its preeminent role during the American Revolution, he dreamed of restoring Virginia's colonial capital to its former glory.

Goodwin felt that historic sites such as Williamsburg were national treasures to be preserved. Not only would they introduce future generations to colonial history but they

would also stand as reminders of the stirring events, principles, and people that fostered the birth of a new nation. Goodwin said, "The best way to look at history is through windows. There are windows here, and there were others, which might be restored, through which unparalleled vistas open into the nation's past."

Goodwin's efforts to enlist support for his vision initially met with little success. Then, in 1926, he persuaded John D. Rockefeller, Jr., heir to the Standard Oil fortune, to tour Williamsburg. Challenged by the opportunity to restore an entire colonial community, Rockefeller agreed to support and fund the project on one condition—that it would encompass the entire town, not just parts of it. His enthusiastic commitment continued for thirty years.

The renaissance of the colonial capital began with the purchase of the Ludwell-Paradise House in 1926. Then the real work began. It was a massive undertaking, because Rockefeller and Goodwin planned more than the mere preservation of historic buildings and settings. They intended to re-create and interpret colonial life as well.

Extensive research was undertaken to ensure historic accuracy throughout the project. Architectural research focused on period maps, deeds, inventories, plans, contemporary drawings, and accounts of the colonial capital. Early photographs documenting the exterior appearances of many of the historic buildings enhanced the restoration efforts.

Perhaps the most important find, however, was an engraved copperplate discovered in the Bodleian Library at Oxford University in England. It was the only known eighteenth-century architectural drawing of colonial Willliamsburg's principal buildings, and it became the basis for the restoration and reconstruction of those structures. In fact, Rockefeller called the Bodleian Plate the "foundation upon which we have based the restoration of the Wren Building and the reconstruction of the Governor's Palace and the Capitol. Without it, we would be acting in the dark; with it, we have gone forward with absolute certainty and conviction."

Meanwhile, archaeological research revealed much about eighteenth-century life. Exploratory cross-trenching unearthed the remains of the Governor's Palace in 1930, including foundation walls, steps, doorways, stone passageways, and the cellar. Additional artifacts discovered there offered guidance for faithfully reconstructing paneling, the hall's black and white marble floor, and other features. Archaeologists also recovered fragments of brick, stone steps, fireplace tiles, hinges, shutter fasteners, locks, and keys. These discoveries and the Bodleian Plate guided the reconstruction of the Governor's Palace on its original eighteenth-century foundations.

Gradually, a picture of everyday eighteenth-century colonial life emerged. Research revealed not only the painstaking craftsmanship of colonial designers and builders but also a new, uniquely American adaptation of classical architectural traditions. In addition, there were insights into the vibrant cultures, lifestyles, and thoughts of colonial residents. They reflected the Age of Enlightenment as well as the Revolutionary concepts of individualism, self-expression, and self-determination that ultimately led to the birth of a vital new nation with a character all its own.

Colonial Williamsburg is now the world's oldest and largest living history museum. The thriving Historic Area, with its knowledgeable, costumed interpreters, offers an opportunity to step back in time and experience a taste of eighteenth-century life. The work begun by the Reverend W. A. R. Goodwin and John D. Rockefeller, Jr., continues today. An endowment established by Rockefeller supports ongoing research and educational programs in the restored colonial capital.

Colonial Williamsburg is a tribute both to the far-sighted, dedicated efforts of the Reverend Goodwin and John D. Rockefeller, Jr., and to the people whose lives they commemorated, the inhabitants of eighteenth-century Williamsburg. Rockefeller himself best described the mammoth restoration effort: "As the work has progressed, I have come to feel that perhaps an even greater value is the lesson that it teaches of the patriotism, high purpose, and unselfish devotion of our forefathers to the common good."

As you walk through historic Williamsburg, remember that it is not just a living museum but a living city as well. Many of the restored and reconstructed homes and outbuildings are residences for Colonial Williamsburg employees; others are hotel facilities. The Historic Area is also the heart of a modern city of approximately twelve thousand residents, which in turn serves a metropolitan area of approximately forty-five thousand people. Colonial Williamsburg is operated by the Colonial Williamsburg Foundation, a nonprofit educational organization. The city is administered by a mayor, council, and city manager.

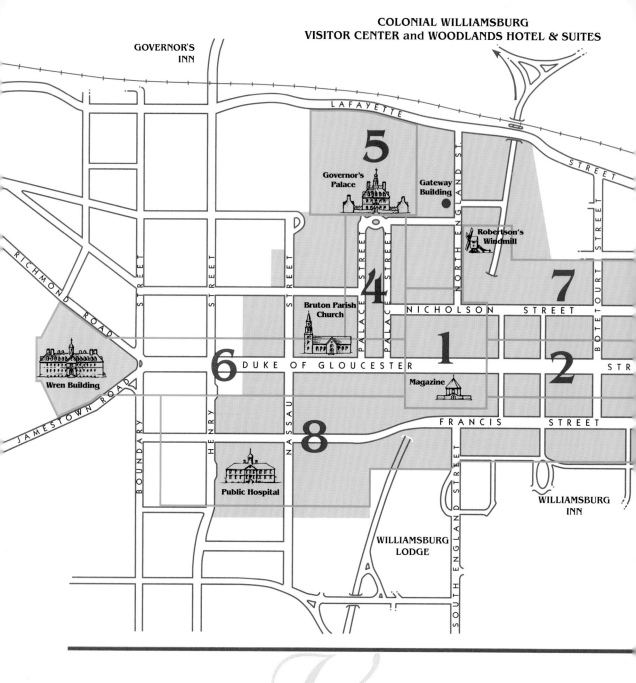

VISITING THE HISTORIC AREA

There is no right or wrong way to visit the Historic Area. Whether you start at the Capitol, the Governor's Palace, or the Shoemaker's Shop, you will find plenty to see and do. Tour every site or concentrate on just a few.

Some sites and activities are centered in and around the Capitol, Governor's Palace, and Peyton Randolph House. Others are scattered throughout the Historic Area. The following is a brief description of what you will find in the restored town. For more information, see

The Historic Area is divided into the following eight geographical areas:

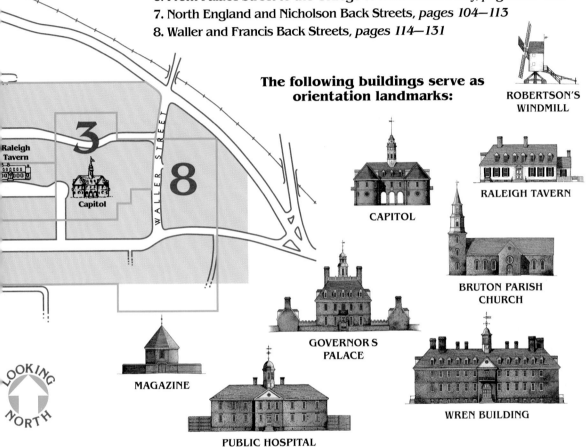

The following buildings serve as orientation landmarks:

ROBERTSON'S WINDMILL

RALEIGH TAVERN

CAPITOL

BRUTON PARISH CHURCH

GOVERNOR'S PALACE

MAGAZINE

WREN BUILDING

PUBLIC HOSPITAL

Raleigh Tavern

Capitol

WALLER STREET

LOOKING NORTH

---

the Street by Street section of this guide.

Check your *Visitor's Companion* to find out which sites are open and which activities are being offered on the day of your visit. The *Visitor's Companion* also lists program times and locations. You may wish to stop by the Gateway Building across from Robertson's Windmill to learn what is happening in the Historic Area and to purchase admission and evening program tickets.

The section numbers correspond to the areas identified on the above map. A ■ *indicates that you need an admission ticket to see an attraction.*

CHECKLIST: DINING AND SHOPPING IN THE HISTORIC AREA

SECTION OF THE HISTORIC AREA	DINING	SHOPPING
1. MARKET SQUARE Near the Courthouse and Magazine	Chowning's Tavern	Market Days on Market Square (open seasonally)
2. FROM MARKET SQUARE TO THE CAPITOL Near the Printing Office and Bookbindery		M. Dubois Grocer Post Office Prentis Store
Near the Raleigh Tavern	King's Arms Tavern Shields Tavern	Golden Ball Raleigh Tavern Bakery Tarpley's Store
3. THE CAPITOL AND ITS SURROUNDINGS Near the Capitol	Christiana Campbell's Tavern	Tickets, Treasures and Books
4–5. AROUND PALACE STREET AND THE GOVERNOR'S PALACE Near the Governor's Palace		McKenzie's Store
6. FROM PALACE STREET TO THE COLLEGE OF WILLIAM AND MARY Near Bruton Parish Church		The Colonial Garden and Nursery (open seasonally) John Greenhow Store Mary Dickinson Store

SECTION 1
MARKET SQUARE

■**Courthouse.** Learn how the colonial legal system affected the lives of ordinary citizens. During presentations of "Order in the Court!" you may become the defendant, a witness, or one of the justices in a reenactment of a real trial from the eighteenth century.

■**Magazine and Guardhouse.** The Magazine served as the arsenal for the Virginia colony. See the authentic firearms and military equipment displayed here and listen as armorers and guards tell the story of British and American military forces in Virginia from the French and Indian War to the War for American Independence.

A replica of a 1750 Newsham patent fire engine is housed in a lean-to on the west wall of the Guardhouse. During warm weather, you may get to help put out a fire by pumping the engine or by serving on the "bucket brigade" to fill it. Special programming is also presented at the Guardhouse.

SECTION 2
FROM MARKET SQUARE TO THE CAPITOL

■**Golden Ball (Silversmith).** Several silversmiths worked in eighteenth century Williamsburg. Today at the

shop of James Craig, you can watch skilled artisans use the tools and methods of their predecessors to create beautiful sterling silver flatware and hollowware.

■**James Anderson Blacksmith Shop.** James Anderson employed several smiths to man his seven forges. He served as public armorer of Virginia before and during the Revolutionary War, and he repaired arms for the American forces. The skilled smiths in this shop today produce tools, nails, fireplace tools, and household furnishings as well as other items for use throughout the Historic Area and around the country.

■**King's Arms Barbershop (Wigmaker).** The wigmaker invites you to his place of business: "To all ladies and gentlemen, we offer all three branches of the trade: wigmaking, barbering, and hairdressing. Using horse, goat, and human hair, our wigmakers craft the finest wigs, curls, and queues for people of fashion. Those so inclined may be pleased that we offer all manner of washing and bathing, along with the finest soaps, perfumes, and powders prepared by the best hands. Counted among our customers are such notables as Thomas Jefferson, Patrick Henry, Peyton Randolph, Thomas Everard, and Peter Pelham."

■**Margaret Hunter Shop (Milliner).** See the milliner and mantua-maker for the latest in London fashions and accessories for the entire family. Choose fabric for a gown. Inquire from Mistress Hunter about having a garment refurbished. Learn how the fashion trades survived the nonimportation agreements and adapted their businesses to the coming Revolution.

■**Mary Stith House.** Enjoy special interpretive programs and encounters with "People of the Past" who portray eighteenth-century citizens.

■**Pasteur & Galt Apothecary Shop.** Do you have an intermittent fever, a toothache, or a broken bone? Visit the shop of apothecary-surgeons Drs. Pasteur and Galt to learn more about eighteenth-century medical theory, treatment, and the preparation of medications.

Printing Office and Bookbindery. Watch as tradesmen use reproduction printing presses to print copies of colonial newspapers, political notices, and manuals. Printed items such as these played a key role in spreading news and information that influenced the choices Virginians made during the years before the Revolution.

Raleigh Tavern. Burgesses and other Virginians gathered at the Raleigh Tavern to discuss the political events that led to revolution. James Southall's tavern also served as a center for social and commercial gatherings— charter members of the Phi Beta Kappa Society met in  the Apollo Room—private and public dinners, lectures and exhibits, and auctions of merchandise, property, and the enslaved. Today at the Raleigh Tavern, you can meet "People of the Past," who portray colonial citizens.

Wetherburn's Tavern. An exhibit in this original building focuses on Henry Wetherburn, his family, and his slaves, who made Wetherburn's Tavern one of the most successful of the 1750s. The outbuildings behind Wetherburn's form a domestic production area essential to the operation of a busy colonial tavern.

SECTION 3
THE CAPITOL AND ITS SURROUNDINGS

Ayscough House (Gunsmith). See gunsmiths fashioning iron, steel, brass, and wood into firearms that are both functional and pleasing to the eye. Discover the importance

---

A WORLD TURNED UPSIDE DOWN

There was a rhythm to life in the late colonial period of Williamsburg's history. Nature governed the flow of the day and established institutions offered a comfortable order that had served the colony well for generations.

By the third quarter of the eighteenth century, all that is changing.

Williamsburg was in the midst of not only a political revolution, but also social, religious, consumer, and technological revolutions. The citizens of Williamsburg and the rest of British America were undergoing fundamental changes in the way they lived their lives. Some of the changes they could control. Others were out of their control. They were living in an era where comfortable traditions were being replaced by new ways.

Today, a journey to Colonial Williamsburg is an opportunity to see how a community dealt with these changes. Tour the home of Peyton Randolph and glimpse what Virginians considered fashionable and what it took to run a household. Sit in the House of Burgesses and wrestle with the same issues that led Virginians to rebel against the most powerful nation in the world. Visit a trade shop and marvel at the technical sophistication craftsmen brought to creating objects. Sit face-to-face with one of our character interpreters and learn about a place where, as the title of a popular tune suggests, *The World Turned Upside Down.*

Programs change from season to season and year to year, so call 1-800-HISTORY before you visit to request a calendar of events. If you have access to the Internet, you can learn about daily and special programming at our Web site, http://www.colonialwilliamsburg.org. Once you are in Williamsburg, check your *Visitor's Companion* for information on programs being offered during your visit.

of rifles, fowling pieces, and muskets to this eighteenth-century community. Learn how gunsmiths such as the Geddys and James Brush provided items from gunlocks to doorlocks in a wide range of materials.

■**Capitol.** Stand in the House of Burgesses and imagine Patrick Henry thundering against British taxation. Decide whether you would have voted for—or against—independence.

■**Public Gaol.** Pirates, murderers, thieves, runaway slaves, suspected loyalists, and debtors inhabited the cells at the Public Gaol (pronounced "jail") at one time or another. Imagine living in this "strong sweet Prison," either as a prisoner or as a member of the family of gaol keeper Peter Pelham.

■**Tickets, Treasures and Books.** This small store offers many historical and nonhistorical publications, games, guest service items, such as cameras and film, as well as operating a ticket office offering admission tickets to all the buildings, carriage rides, and evening programs. The staff of the shop is willing and able to direct guests and answer questions regarding their visit to the historic sites, availability of tickets for special programs, and make dining reservations.

SECTION 4
AROUND PALACE STREET

■**George Wythe House.**
Visit the home of Thomas Jefferson's teacher and friend. George Wythe was a prominent attorney, burgess, clerk of the House of Burgesses, signer of the Declaration of Independence, framer of the U. S. Constitution, professor of law, and judge.

See demonstrations of down hearth cooking in the kitchen behind the house.

■**Thomas Everard House.** An exhibit features the lives of widower Thomas Everard, his two daughters, and nineteen slaves. Everard arrived in Virginia as an orphan apprentice in the 1730s and rose to the positions of clerk of the York County Court, mayor of Williamsburg, member of the Bruton Parish Church vestry, and deputy clerk of the General Court.

■**Play Booth Theater** (open seasonally). Enjoy scenes from plays performed in Williamsburg in the years immediately before the American Revolution.

SECTION 5
THE GOVERNOR'S PALACE

■**Governor's Palace.** Tour the elegant and imposing residence of seven royal governors. From the weaponry display in the entrance hall to the royal portraits in the ballroom,  the Governor's Palace was meant to impress visitors with the prestige and power of the king's representative in Virginia. During the Revolution, the first two governors of the Commonwealth of Virginia, Patrick Henry and Thomas Jefferson, also lived here.

Explore the beautiful gardens, then visit the kitchen to see demonstrations of eighteenth-century cooking techniques and to learn about dining customs and kitchen duties.

■**Wheelwright.** In the eighteenth century, there was a demand for wheeled vehicles of every kind—wheelbarrows, riding chairs, carriages, and carts. Today, the wheelwrights construct and repair the vehicles used throughout the Historic Area, from riding chairs to cannon carriages.

SECTION 6
FROM PALACE STREET TO THE COLLEGE OF WILLIAM AND MARY

Bruton Parish Church . There was no separation of church and state in colonial Virginia. The Church of England was the official religion for the colony, and, as the Anglican church in the capital, Bruton Parish Church was probably the most important church in Virginia. This Episcopal church has been in use since 1715 and serves an active congregation today.

The Colonial Garden and Nursery (open seasonally). Learn about eighteenth-century horticultural practices, then purchase plants and supplies to create your own colonial-style garden.

■**James Geddy House and Foundry.** This house served as the residence, workshop, and shop for silversmith James Geddy, Jr. Learn about the domestic and business life of the Geddy family.

In the foundry behind the house, watch skilled craftsmen cast objects in bronze, brass, pewter, and silver.

■**Shoemaker's Shop.** The shoemaker made plain and fancy shoes and boots for gentlemen. Watch as tradesmen hand-sew shoes with "good thread well twisted" and stitches that are "hard drawn with handleathers," as one colonial Virginia statute prescribed.

■**Taliaferro-Cole Shop (Harnessmaker-**

Saddler). Leather was one of the most useful raw materials in the eighteenth century. Today, tradesmen make harnesses, saddles, leather water buckets, and other useful goods.

EVENING PROGRAMS

There's almost as much to do at Colonial Williamsburg at night as there is during the day. Experience the life of the common soldier at the Magazine. Engage in festivities at the Raleigh Tavern or laugh at the antics of a traveling troupe of entertainers at the Courthouse. Attend a candlelit concert at the Governor's Palace. Decide the innocence or guilt of the "Virginia Witch." Hear tales of the unexplained as you walk through the long shadows of Williamsburg after dark.

Call 1-800-HISTORY to purchase your evening program tickets before your visit. You can read about evening programs on our Web site, http://www.colonialwilliamsburg.org, if you have access to the Internet.

In Williamsburg, you can buy evening program tickets at the Visitor Center, Gateway Building, Lumber House ticket office, Secretary's Office, Merchants Square Ticket Office, or your hotel. Check your *Visitor's Companion* for more information.

Wren Building. The Wren Building is the oldest academic building still in use in America. Learn about the important role the  College of William and Mary played in the intellectual life of the Virginia colony and the extraordinary number of distinguished alumni, including Thomas Jefferson, John Marshall, and James Monroe, it nurtured.

SECTION 7
NORTH ENGLAND AND NICHOLSON BACK STREETS

■**Brickmaker's Yard** (open seasonally). Watch and perhaps help as brickmakers tread clay and mold bricks to be fired in a kiln. Although brickyards like this one would have been familiar to eighteenth-century residents, bricks were often made at or near building sites.

■**Carpenter.** It took about as much time to erect a house in eighteenth-century Williamsburg as it does today, assuming you count only construction hours and not those required to prepare the building materials. Today, carpenters are preparing materials and reconstructing outbuildings behind the Peyton Randolph House.

■**Cooper.** Watch coopers shape and assemble staves to form casks, piggins, and other wooden containers. In an age without cardboard boxes or plastic buckets, people used products made by the cooper in their  homes and businesses—including churns to make butter, buckets to carry water, piggins to scoop things out of larger containers, and casks to store and ship cider, grain, and tobacco.

■**Hay's Cabinetmaking Shop (Cabinetmaker).** Visit the wareroom—a combination showroom and warehouse—where the cabinetmaker met his customers and conducted the majority of his business. Then go to the workroom and watch the master, journeymen, and apprentices use the hand tools and technology of the colonial era to produce furniture, harpsichords, and spinets.

■**Peyton Randolph House.** What did "revolution" mean to the residents of this stately home? To Speaker of the House of Burgesses Peyton Randolph, it meant leading the patriot movement in Virginia and eventually in Philadelphia, where he served as president of the first and second Continental Congresses. To Peyton's wife, Betty, it meant coping with the British occupation of Williamsburg in 1781. To several of the Randolph slaves, it meant a chance for freedom by running away to the British.

■**Robertson's Windmill.** Wind-driven  stones that grind corn. Colonial Virginians depended on local mills to grind the grain from which they made their bread, a staple of their diet that appeared at nearly every meal.

■**Rural Trades.** See such eighteenth-century farm and country life activities as cider making and basketmaking. Explore fields and pastures planted with corn, wheat, tobacco, and other field crops.

■**Tenant House.** Visit with "People of the Past" portraying the "lesser sort" of Williamsburg residents. The Tenant House features the stories of working-class people who tried to make their livelihoods in the capital city. They rented modest dwellings and sought employment wherever they could find it. Some found success; others did not.

CHILDREN'S ACTIVITIES

Children can satisfy their curiosity year-round at Colonial Williamsburg. Let your offspring try on shackles at the Public Gaol, testify at an eighteenth-century trial, train with the military, or make friends with the farm animals throughout the Historic Area.

Summer provides even more opportunities for young time travelers to enjoy the past. Your children might learn the latest (circa 1775) country dance, help out in a garden, play trapball, or draw water from a well. They can talk with children in costume about what it would have been like to live in Williamsburg right before the American Revolution. Boys and girls can rent costumes and "become" colonial children. Some children's programming also is available during holiday weekends and many weekends in the spring and fall. Look especially for programs at the James Geddy and Benjamin Powell Houses.

Check at the Visitor Center or the Gateway Building during your visit to learn which sites and activities in the Historic Area will appeal to your children. Look for the 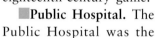 symbol in your *Visitor's Companion* to find family programs.

SECTION 8
WALLER AND FRANCIS
BACK STREETS

■**Bassett Hall.** Take a tour of the eighteenth-century house that Mr. and Mrs. John D. Rockefeller, Jr., adapted for their Williamsburg home. The house remains much as it was when the Rockefellers restored it and furnished it from the mid-1930s onward. You can also tour the garden, which still blooms in the spring and in the fall, just as it did to mark the Rockefellers' seasonal visits.

■**Benjamin Powell House** (open seasonally). Experience everyday life in a middling

colonial household. Your children might help make the bed, prepare dinner, weed the garden, or learn an eighteenth-century game.

■**Public Hospital.** The Public Hospital was the first public institution in British North America devoted exclusively to the care and treatment of the mentally ill. See how the treatment of mental disorders changed from 1773, when the hospital opened, through 1885, when a fire destroyed the colonial buildings. The Public Hospital serves as the entrance to the DeWitt Wallace Decorative Arts Museum.

■**DeWitt Wallace Decorative Arts Museum.** A description of the Museum begins on page 135.

CHECKLIST: DINING AND SHOPPING WITHIN WALKING DISTANCE OF THE HISTORIC AREA

SECTION OF THE HISTORIC AREA	DINING	SHOPPING
8. FRANCIS STREET Near the Magazine	Golden Horseshoe Gold Course Clubhouse Williamsburg Inn Williamsburg Lodge	Craft House at the Williamsburg Inn Golden Horseshoe Gold Course Golf Pro Shop Golden Horseshoe Green Course Pro Shop Abby Aldrich Rockefeller Folk Art Museum Gift Shop Regency Gift Shop at the Williamsburg Inn Tidewater Shop at the Williamsburg Lodge
Near the Wren Building	Merchants Square Wallace Museum Café	Craft House at Merchants Square Everything Williamsburg The DeWitt Wallace Decorative Arts Museum Gift Shop WILLIAMSBURG Pure Simple Today

WASHINGTON, HENRY, AND JEFFERSON IN WILLIAMSBURG

Williamsburg was a training ground for George Washington, Patrick Henry, and Thomas Jefferson. Each came here as a young man, and each matured here as a statesman.

 George Washington's first known trip to Williamsburg was in 1752, when he met Governor Dinwiddie for the first time. Late that year, Dinwiddie commissioned the young man adjutant of the Southern District of Virginia. Washington attracted further public notice in 1754, when he returned to Williamsburg after completing a dangerous mission to the Ohio country at Dinwiddie's request. This feat launched the twenty-one-year-old Washington's military career, which he later parlayed into a seat in the House of Burgesses. His experiences during his sixteen years as a burgess—negotiating legislation in committee rooms, engaging in political discussions in Williamsburg's homes and taverns, forging social and political relationships—helped mold him into a political leader.

 Patrick Henry first traveled to Williamsburg in 1760 to obtain a law license. Although the twenty-three-year-old applicant barely squeaked through the examination conducted by George Wythe, John and Peyton Randolph, and Robert Carter Nicholas, he left the city with his license. Henry began making a name for himself as an attorney and gained even greater fame when, as a first-time burgess, he led Virginia's opposition to the Stamp Act in 1765. His impassioned "Caesar had . . . his Brutus" speech provoked cries of treason from the other legislators, but the House adopted most of Henry's resolutions against the Stamp Act. For the next eleven years, Henry's ringing oratory—including his immortal cry, "give me liberty or give me death!"—rallied Virginians to the patriot cause.

 Seventeen-year-old Thomas Jefferson arrived in Williamsburg in 1760 to attend the College of William and Mary. As the cousin of John and Peyton Randolph, he had immediate entrée to Williamsburg society. After two years at William and Mary, Jefferson began reading law under George Wythe. He also attended the courts and legislative sessions at the Capitol and was standing near the door of the House of Burgesses when Henry delivered his Caesar–Brutus speech.

Jefferson was elected to the House of Burgesses in 1769. His first session was as eventful as Henry's had been four years earlier. After Governor Botetourt dissolved the legislature for protesting the Townshend Acts, the burgesses met at the Raleigh Tavern and drew up a nonimportation agreement. Jefferson signed the agreement, as did Washington and Henry.

In the years that followed, all three men supported the patriot cause and the nation that grew out of it. Each represented Virginia at the Continental Congress in Philadelphia, although not at the same time. Washington led the American forces to victory over the British and guided the country as our first president. Henry served as the first governor of the state of Virginia, eventually holding that office four times. Jefferson wrote the Declaration of Independence, succeeded Henry as governor, and ultimately served as president of the United States.

COLONIAL WILLIAMSBURG STREET BY STREET

The following pages discuss the history of the buildings and sites in the Historic Area as well as "Becoming Americans," the interpretative basis for the story we tell at Colonial Williamsburg. The section numbers correspond to those on the map on pages 24–25. Each section contains one or more detailed maps, drawings of the buildings, and character sketches that are based on real people and combine fact and conjecture. An asterisk (*) indicates that a building is an original eighteenth- or nineteenth-century structure, and a ■ indicates that you need an admission ticket to see an attraction.

You can tour each section of the Historic Area independently and in any order. Each area map's symbols will enable you to identify and locate the following:

- Exhibits requiring a ticket
- Original buildings
- Places to shop
- Places to dine
- Exhibition gardens
- Information and ticket sales sites
- Rest rooms
- Cold drinks
- Water fountains
- Public telephones
- Other services and places to visit
- Facilities accessible to persons with disabilities

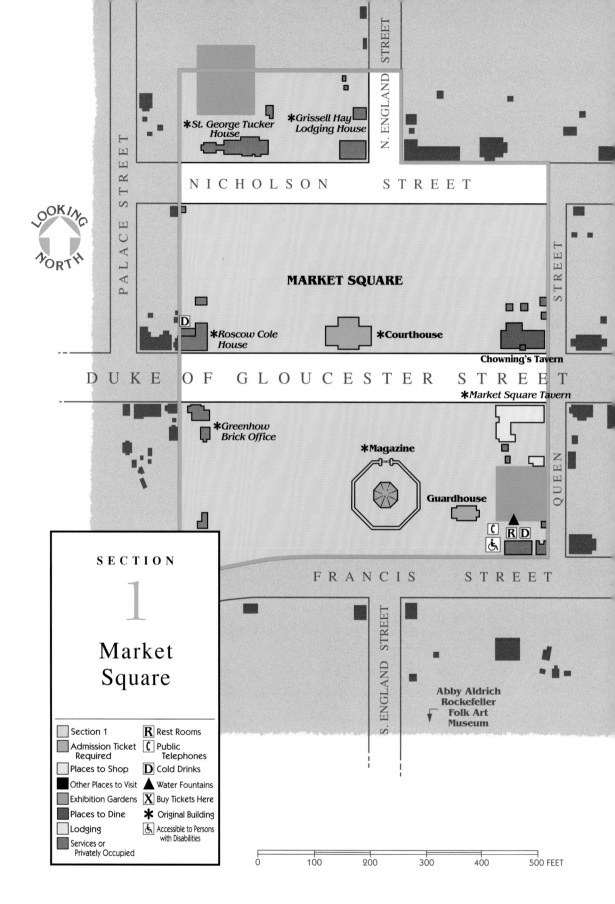

LOOKING NORTH

PALACE STREET

N. ENGLAND STREET

*St. George Tucker House

*Grissell Hay Lodging House

NICHOLSON STREET

MARKET SQUARE

STREET

D

*Roscow Cole House

*Courthouse

Chowning's Tavern

DUKE OF GLOUCESTER STREET

*Market Square Tavern

*Greenhow Brick Office

*Magazine

Guardhouse

C
♿

R D

QUEEN STREET

FRANCIS STREET

S. ENGLAND STREET

Abby Aldrich Rockefeller Folk Art Museum

SECTION

1

Market Square

Section 1	**R** Rest Rooms
Admission Ticket Required	**C** Public Telephones
Places to Shop	**D** Cold Drinks
Other Places to Visit	▲ Water Fountains
Exhibition Gardens	**X** Buy Tickets Here
Places to Dine	✳ Original Building
Lodging	♿ Accessible to Persons with Disabilities
Services or Privately Occupied	

0   100   200   300   400   500 FEET

MARKET SQUARE

An asterisk (*) indicates that a building is an original eighteenth- or nineteenth-century structure. A ▪ indicates that you need an admission ticket to see an attraction.

arket Square, a green open space about halfway between the College of William and Mary and the Capitol, was set aside as a permanent area for markets and fairs by an act of the General Assembly early in the eighteenth century.

There, before dawn on each market day—as often as six times a week later in the century—the town slowly came alive. People from nearby farms brought produce in creaking wagons or carts. Sometimes cattle and sheep competed for road space leading to the square, driven on by shouting children and yelping dogs. In the predawn light, vendors unloaded meat, eggs, milk, butter, fish, crabs, oysters, fruit, and vegetables, displaying their wares on makeshift counters of pine boards.

Armed with lists of the provisions needed for the day, housewives, cooks, and kitchen slaves selected the freshest eggs, the ripest peaches, and the choicest cuts of meat. Shopping was an everyday chore in an age without refrigeration.

By midmorning, most of the produce had been sold or looked shopworn. The crowds began to melt away. Some of the farmers repaired to one of the taverns conveniently located next to the square to relax, listen to the local gossip, and quench their thirst.

The Williamsburg charter of 1722 established two fairs each year, one on April 23, the feast of St. George, the patron saint of England, and the other on December 12. A variety of merchandise, including livestock, was sold on the square. People enjoyed games, puppet shows, horse races, cockfights, dancing and fiddling for prizes, and a chase for a "Pig, with the Tail soap'd."

Auctions of the enslaved, goods, and land occurred on Market Square. After Josiah Chowning's death in 1772, for example, some property that he owned and one of his slaves were auctioned off in front of the Courthouse—within sight of the tavern that bears his name.

Market Square was also important as a seat of local government. In 1715, the courthouse for James City County fronted on Market Square. The present structure, built at the center of the square in 1770, housed both the municipal and the county courts until 1932. In all, a local government building stood on or adjacent to the square for more than two hundred years.

Near the Courthouse was the training field for the Williamsburg Militia Company, which mustered there several times a year. With a few exceptions, the colonial militia consisted of every free, white, able-bodied man, aged sixteen to sixty, who was a British subject. A militia muster brought together members of different social classes without leveling social distinctions. Musters formalized and validated the authority figures in colonial society, the large landowners who were appointed to command the militia and who served without pay. Those officers deemed military service both an honor and an obligation, and they could be fined as much as twenty pounds for failure to perform. By contrast, three shillings was the typical fine for an absent militiaman.

Much of the rest of the local population turned out to watch the training and drills in quick loading and shooting. All was not marching and manual-of-arms practice, however. Militiamen participated in foot races, wrestling matches, and cudgeling standoffs, with prizes being awarded to the victors. Afterward, the officers might treat the entire company to a hogshead of rum punch.

Market Square's central location made it a favorite place for public notices, official announcements, communal celebrations, and elections. In July 1746, a large bonfire was lit and the public consumed three barrels of punch in honor of the Duke of Cumberland's

MEET . . . JANE MOODY

Early mornings found Jane Moody and other middling housewives shopping for their households in Market Square. They purchased milk, butter, vegetables, fruits, fresh meats, and other foodstuffs. Because Jane and her husband, Matthew, kept a tavern at their house, she had to buy supplies for both her family and their customers.

Running a tavern was much like managing a home, only on a larger scale. The Moodys' house on Capitol Landing Road was nearly always crowded with tavern customers, usually travelers waiting for or just arrived on the ferry from Gloucester County that Matthew Moody operated. Four slaves did the heaviest work. The two women, Thomasin and Rachel, saw to most of the cooking and cleaning. Cutty and London took care of customers' horses and helped with the ferry service. Sometimes Matthew hired ferrymen to assist him. Occasionally his grown-up sons pitched in to keep the family business going.

Responsibilities for operating the tavern fell mostly to Jane these days. No longer the lively sixty-year-old widower she had married, Matthew was getting on in years now. Jane found it both convenient and reassuring that her stepsons Philip, Ishmael, William, and Matthew, Jr., lived nearby. Her stepsons were kind to her and solicitous of their aging father, and Jane felt no resentment toward them. She wished her own children could help, but they lived too far away.

Jane enjoyed living in Williamsburg. In addition to the convenience of the twice-weekly market, town life offered other advantages. Once in a while, Jane drank tea with her women friends in her neighborhood. She visited Mr. Greenhow's store to purchase necessities for the house and tavern as well as the occasional luxury for herself—a skein of silk or a handkerchief. When Matthew was not feeling well, he could consult one of several local doctors. Jane looked forward to worshiping at Bruton Parish Church, her major consolation. Before and after Sunday services, she enjoyed chatting with acquaintances.

Although Jane occasionally longed for a quiet moment to call her own, she knew how lucky she was to have an honest husband, helpful relatives close at hand, a profitable business, and a good roof over her head.

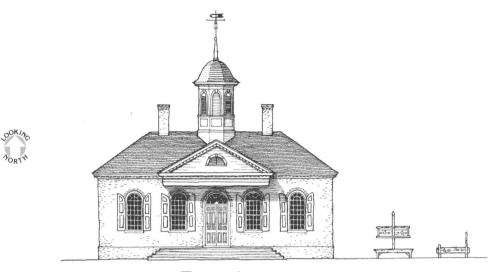

■ *Courthouse*

victory over Bonnie Prince Charlie at the battle of Culloden. On July 25, 1776, attorney Benjamin Waller proclaimed the Declaration of Independence from the Courthouse steps to a huge throng after the news arrived from Philadelphia.

Elections were public affairs in colonial Virginia. Voters gathered at the Courthouse to choose the men who would serve as their representatives in the House of Burgesses.

Market Square's convenient location must have been paramount in the decision to keep the town's fire engine, which was in use by 1756, there. Fire was a constant hazard in the eighteenth century. An efficient response to the threat of fire required organization and cooperation.

Market Square is dominated by the ■Courthouse. Built in 1770–1771, the Courthouse was the meeting place for the James City County Court, the Hustings Court (the municipal court for the city of Williamsburg), and the mayor and aldermen of the City Council for more than 150 years. Like many other Virginia courthouses, it is T-shaped. Its formal design elements—round-headed windows, a cantilevered pediment,

and an octagonal cupola with the original weather vane—add to and reinforce the building's official appearance.

In colonial Virginia, the county court was the principal agent of local government and had broad executive and judicial authority. Its jurisdiction included crimes ranging from petty theft to absence from church. Free subjects of the king accused of felonies were sent on to the General Court, which met in the Capitol; slaves were tried locally for the same crimes. Both were sometimes publicly hanged as a warning to others. The municipal court, known as the "Hustings Court," possessed the civil jurisdiction within the city of Wil-

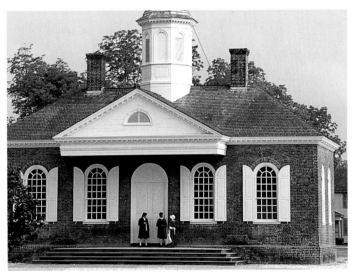

Roscow Cole House

liamsburg that the James City County Court exercised in the adjacent county.

The Hustings Court met on the first Monday of each month, and the James City County Court convened on the second Monday. Sessions lasted several days until the backlog of cases was cleared.

The onlookers who often filled the Courthouse to overflowing on court days got their fill of debtor and creditor tales, card cheaters, pig stealers, and more. The theatricality of the proceedings was heightened because convicted offenders were usually punished immediately after the verdict. Often their sentence included public flogging at the whipping post conveniently located just outside the Courthouse. Petty offenders were locked in the stocks or pillory, where they were exposed to public ridicule and abuse.

The ■**Magazine** was erected in 1715 after Lieutenant Governor Alexander Spotswood urgently requested a "good substantial house of brick" in which to store the arms and ammunition dispatched from London for the defense of the colony. Governor Spotswood himself is credited with the Magazine's unusual octagonal design.

The Magazine assumed added importance during the French and Indian War, 1754–1763, when for the first time the colony supported large-scale military operations in the Ohio Valley, territory that the Crown claimed under the Virginia charter of 1609. Because the amount of gunpowder in storage exceeded sixty thousand pounds, the residents of Williamsburg felt that the Magazine needed further protection. A high wall was therefore built around the Magazine and a ■**Guardhouse** was constructed nearby.

At its busiest, the Magazine probably contained two to three thousand Brown Bess muskets and enough shot, powder, and flints to equip a formidable army. Other military equipment—tents, tools, swords, pikes, canteens, and cooking utensils—was also stored in the Magazine.

During the night of April 20–21, 1775, British sailors acting on Governor Dunmore's orders removed gunpowder from the Magazine. Although violence was averted, the Gunpowder Incident helped move Virginians toward revolution.

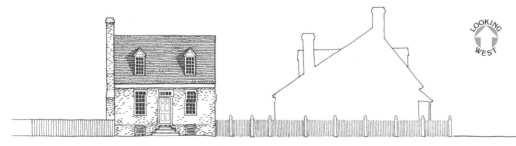

Greenhow Brick Office

After the Revolution, an arsenal at Williamsburg was no longer needed, although the Confederate forces did store powder in the Magazine during the Civil War. The building was later used as a market, a Baptist meetinghouse, a dancing school, and finally as a livery stable.

The Association for the Preservation of Virginia Antiquities made the safeguarding of the Magazine its first project. In 1986, Colonial Williamsburg obtained the Magazine from the A.P.V.A.

Directly west of the Magazine is the **Greenhow Brick Office.** Although Williamsburg was the port of entry for the upper James River, there was no customhouse in town, a situation much belabored by the inspector general of customs when he visited in 1760. Accounts indicate that a public building, "located in the square" on municipal property, existed by 1764. It is likely that this modest brick structure was used as the Williamsburg customhouse.

The brick portion of the **Roscow Cole House** was erected in 1812 to face Market Square by Roscow Cole, a local merchant. The westerly wooden frame section is a reconstruction of an eighteenth-century building. An 1830 insurance policy called this structure a dry goods store.

The **St. George Tucker House** belonged to noted jurist St. George Tucker, who attended the College of William and Mary and later became professor of law there. Tucker bought the property in 1788. He moved an older

The "bucket brigade" fills the colonial fire engine with water.

building, which had faced Palace green, to this site, enlarged the house, and reoriented it toward Market Square.

Today the St. George Tucker House is Colonial Williamsburg's donor reception center. Through the generosity of Mr. and Mrs. James W. Gorman, Ms. Marilyn Brown and Mr. Douglas N. Morton, and an anonymous donor, the house has been restored to its eigh-

■ *Guardhouse*

■ **Magazine*

St. George Tucker House

teenth-century appearance and redecorated with period reproductions. At the Tucker House, conveniently located in the Historic Area, donors to the Foundation can rest and enjoy light refreshments. The staff assists with reservations and information about Colonial Williamsburg. Guests also enjoy visiting with other friends of the Foundation.

■ **PEYTON RANDOLPH HOUSE.** A description of the Peyton Randolph House begins on page 105.

The **Grissell Hay Lodging House** to the east may be one of the first houses on Market Square. The core of the house may date from around 1720, when it belonged to Dr. Archibald Blair, a Scottish physician and a partner in Williamsburg's leading mercantile business, the Prentis Store. The present exterior probably dates from the second half of the eighteenth century. Apothecary Peter Hay, whose shop on Duke of Gloucester Street burned in 1756, lived here in the 1760s. After Hay's death, his widow, Grissell, operated the dwelling as a lodging house. Widows who needed to support themselves and their chil-

dren often kept lodging houses (the equivalents of today's bed-and-breakfasts).

Chowning's Tavern stands east of the Courthouse. In 1766, Josiah Chowning advertised the opening of his tavern "where all who please to favour me with their custom may depend on the best of entertainment for themselves, servants, and horses, and good pasturage." Chowning's Tavern serves hearty fare similar to the dishes enjoyed by its patrons in the eighteenth century.

Across the street, **Market Square Tavern** has been a hostelry for more than two hundred years. Its most celebrated lodger was Thomas Jefferson, who rented rooms there from Thomas Craig, tailor, while he studied law under George Wythe. Neither Chowning's nor Market Square Tavern, however, could compete with the more profitable establishments farther east down Duke of Gloucester Street toward the Capitol. Today Market Square Tavern and the Market Square Tavern Kitchen are two of several Colonial Williamsburg hotel facilities located in the Historic Area.

Chowning's Tavern

Grissell Hay Lodging House

Becoming Americans
Our Struggle to Be Both Free and Equal

FAMILY LIFE

In the 1700s, changes in traditional family structures affected the way family members defined themselves in relation to one another and to society. Ultimately, these changes created the pattern for the "modern American" family.

Adverse conditions in seventeenth-century Virginia made it difficult for European and African immigrants to form stable family structures but began to ease by the late 1600s. Native American families, however, continued to be undermined by disease, displacement, and warfare.

The European family was modeled after a patriarchal ideal that placed the father in a position of supreme authority over an extended family. Reality often differed from the ideal. Enslaved Africans, torn from their homelands and denied the stability of legal marriage, created distinctively African-Virginian family structures that relied on African concepts of extended kinships. European observers misunderstood the traditional patterns of Native American work and family relationships. Interaction with Europeans further altered the family structure of Native American families and ultimately threatened their very survival.

A more openly affectionate, child-centered family that reflected egalitarian republican sentiment and changing roles for men and women began to emerge in gentry and middling white families in the late 1700s. This redefined structure became part of the ideal for the new American nation, yet lack of opportunity continued for some white, Native American, and black families.

Market Square Tavern

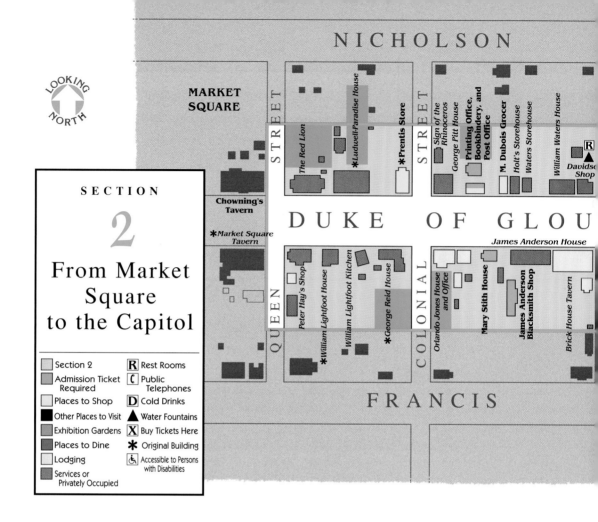

NICHOLSON

MARKET SQUARE

STREET

The Red Lion

*Ludwell-Paradise House

*Prentis Store

STREET

Sign of the Rhinoceros

George Pitt House

Printing Office, Bookbindery, and Post Office

M. Dubois Grocer

Holt's Storehouse

Waters Storehouse

William Waters House

R

Davidso Shop

Chowning's Tavern

*Market Square Tavern

DUKE OF GLOU

James Anderson House

QUEEN

Peter Hay's Shop

*William Lightfoot House

William Lightfoot Kitchen

*George Reid House

COLONIAL

Orlando Jones House and Office

Mary Stith House

James Anderson Blacksmith Shop

Brick House Tavern

FRANCIS

SECTION

2

From Market Square to the Capitol

☐ Section 2	**R** Rest Rooms
☐ Admission Ticket Required	**C** Public Telephones
☐ Places to Shop	**D** Cold Drinks
■ Other Places to Visit	▲ Water Fountains
☐ Exhibition Gardens	**X** Buy Tickets Here
■ Places to Dine	✱ Original Building
☐ Lodging	♿ Accessible to Persons with Disabilities
☐ Services or Privately Occupied	

FROM MARKET SQUARE TO THE CAPITOL

An asterisk (*) indicates that a building is an original eighteenth- or nineteenth-century structure. A ■ indicates that you need an admission ticket to see an attraction.

Attracted by the numerous opportunities to eat, drink, or socialize, or perhaps to purchase the latest goods from London or a newspaper or book, most eighteenth-century townsfolk and visitors to the colonial capital found their way "downtown" on Duke of Gloucester Street.

The three blocks of Duke of Gloucester Street from Market Square eastward to the Capitol were the busiest in eighteenth-century Williamsburg. General stores and specialty shops offered a wide range of goods at prices that ordinary consumers could afford. A number of taverns provided food, drink, and accommodations to an increasingly mobile and widely traveled public. In 1765, one visitor described the scene: "In the Day time people hurrying back and forwards from the Capitoll

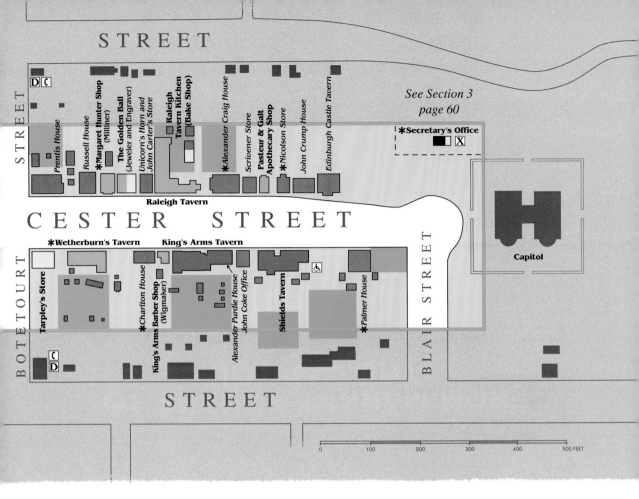

*See Section 3
page 60*

to the taverns, and at night, Carousing and Drinking in one Chamber and box and Dice in another, which Continues till morning."

Today, these same blocks of Duke of Gloucester Street appear more neatly residential than they would have two hundred years ago, when many of the houses served interchangeably as shops, stores, taverns, and residences, and the street bustled with mercantile activity. Lots at the end of the street nearest the Capitol had the most commercial character. They increased in value and often were subdivided as retailers and tavern keepers jostled for a location in this popular area.

William Parks, the first public printer in the colony of Virginia, began the weekly *Virginia Gazette* in 1736. Williamsburg thus became a communications center as news of the world, of the colony, and of the city provided essential information to those whose affairs depended more and more on the "freshest advices" from far and near.

Light industry also developed at the back of the James Anderson property, where Anderson established a blacksmithing operation. Anderson served as public armorer of Virginia before and during the Revolutionary War, and he repaired arms for the American forces.

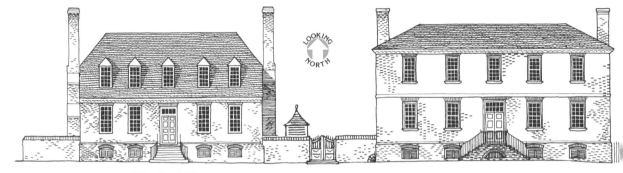

The Red Lion

*Ludwell-Paradise House

FROM MARKET SQUARE TO COLONIAL STREET

This part of Duke of Gloucester Street was less commercially attractive than the east end because it was farther away from the Capitol. As a result, the block's half-acre lots were never subdivided. **The Red Lion** on the left suffered many failures and a rapid turnover of its tavern keepers, including Josiah Chowning at one time.

The haystack sign announces **Peter Hay's Shop.** Apothecary Hay fared somewhat better as a businessman than did his neighbors across the street until April 1756, when the *Maryland Gazette* reported that a fire broke out in his shop "and in less than Half an Hour entirely consumed the same, together with all Medicines, Utensils, & c." Fortunately, "the Assistance of a Fire Engine" prevented damage to nearby buildings. The kitchen behind the shop now houses Colonial Williamsburg hotel guests.

The **Ludwell-Paradise House** is an example of the mixed use of buildings over time. Al-

though an earlier structure existed on this site, the present dwelling was built by Philip Ludwell III about 1755. In Williamsburg, space meant money, so even this elegant town house was rented as a tenement for many years. William Rind—and later his widow, Clementina—operated a press on the premises. Ludwell's eccentric daughter, Lucy Ludwell Paradise, lived here in the 1800s. The Ludwell-Paradise House was the first property purchased by John D. Rockefeller, Jr.

The **William Lightfoot House and Kitchen** on the south side of the street belonged to a Yorktown merchant whose business apparently brought him to Williamsburg so often that he felt the need for a local dwelling.

The **George Reid House** may have been built as late as 1790 by a merchant who operated a store near the Capitol. Archaeological excavations revealed that a path near the house was paved with fragments of clay pipes that might have been broken in shipment to Williamsburg. Matching pieces have also been found at the Prentis Store across the street.

The **Prentis Store** is Williamsburg's best

*George Reid House

William Lightfoot Kitchen

*William Lightfoot House

Prentis Store

surviving example of a colonial store. The firm of Prentis and Company operated a highly successful general store in this handsome original building from 1740 until the Revolution. The tea shipment that Yorktown patriots threw into the York River during their tea party of 1774 was consigned to this firm.

A classic example of store architecture, its gable end faced the street. Through the door above, merchandise could easily be lifted into the loft. Windows along the sides were located toward the rear of the building to light the counting room and to leave long, blank walls for ample shelving in the sales area.

The Prentis Store dates from 1739 to 1740. It survived into the twentieth century as a gas station, which partially explains why so few changes were made to its fabric; it was likely considered "beneath" modernization or conversion. Prentis himself lived a block away in a substantial house at the corner of Botetourt and Duke of Gloucester Streets, where he spent his leisure hours planning and planting a fine garden. Goods like those sold in eighteenth-century stores are available at Prentis Store.

Peter Hay's Shop

MEET . . .
CLEMENTINA RIND

Clementina Rind (1740–1774) was the editor of the *Virginia Gazette* from 1773 to 1774. She also ran a printing business and acted as publisher for the House of Burgesses, which meant that she was the first woman to operate such an enterprise in the colony. A widow, Clementina had five children. Her home and her printing business were both located in the Ludwell-Paradise House.

Clementina came to Williamsburg from Annapolis, Maryland, with her husband, William. He established a second newspaper in Williamsburg. When William died in August 1773, Clementina assumed the editorship without missing a single issue of the paper.

The result was a newspaper that closely followed her personal tastes. She printed news with a decidedly feminine slant. For example, instead of publishing the usual formal address when the governor's wife arrived in February 1774, Clementina printed a poem emphasizing peace and contentment around Lord and Lady Dunmore's hearth.

Clementina Rind died on September 25, 1774.

Sign of the Rhinoceros *George Pitt House* ◼ *Printing Office, Post Office, and Bookbindery* *M. Dubois Grocer*

FROM COLONIAL STREET TO BOTETOURT STREET

Although the **George Pitt House** was built as a residence, it sometimes served as a combination shop and dwelling in the eighteenth century. Sarah Packe, a young widow, had her millinery business here and also took in lodgers. Later, Dr. George Pitt purchased the property and opened an apothecary shop, the Sign of the Rhinoceros. Dr. Pitt sold the property to printer John Dixon in 1774.

Next door, the ◼**Printing Office, Post Office, and Bookbindery** were the town's communications hub. The boxlike protruding windows decorated with the most recent prints from England not only proclaimed the latest fashions but helped to create a demand for them. Reading was recognized as an important element in commerce. The newspapers, prints, magazines, Bibles, and inexpensive books on every conceivable subject available

here fueled the great information explosion of the eighteenth century.

William Parks published the *Virginia Gazette,* the first newspaper printed in the colony, from 1736 to 1750. He also became "public printer" to the General Assembly and the colony's first postmaster. Parks established a paper mill just outside Williamsburg—"the first Mill of the Kind, that ever was erected in this Colony." In that venture, he had the advice and backing of a fellow printer, Benjamin Franklin, who later purchased paper from Parks's mill.

Several hundred pieces of type, probably Dutch, were unearthed at this site during archaeological excavations that also uncovered bookbinder's ornaments and crucibles in which Parks may have melted lead. Archaeologists also found lead border ornaments used in printing paper money during the French and Indian War.

The next three structures—**M. Dubois Grocer, Holt's Storehouse,** and **Waters Storehouse**—form a fine collection of reconstructed eighteenth-century commercial properties, all of which present their gable ends to the street.

Tenant grocer M. Dubois occupied this store in the late 1770s. Today, M. Dubois Grocer carries food products such as Virginia ham, peanuts, condiments, preserves, cheese biscuits, and beverages.

The three sugar loaves hanging outside Holt's Storehouse are the traditional sign of the grocer. In addition to groceries, John Holt sold dry goods and china.

Holt's
Storehouse

Waters
Storehouse

William Waters House

Davidson Shop

Storekeepers tried to stock a wide range of products, especially yard goods and iron tools. Customers were hard to attract and harder to keep. One local merchant wrote to his Scottish supplier imploring him to send a variety of merchandise, lest the shopkeeper lose the goodwill of his customers: "I find there will be an Absollute Necessity of allways [having] a good assortment in order to keep my Customers entirely to myself without allowing them to go to my neighbours for trifles."

The reconstructed **William Waters House** is named for the wealthy planter from the Eastern Shore who bought the dwelling for his house in town when he moved to Williamsburg about 1750.

The **Davidson Shop** on the corner was once the apothecary shop of Robert Davidson, a "Practitioner in Physick" and mayor of Williamsburg in 1738.

Orlando Jones, born in 1681, owned the original **Orlando Jones House and Office**

on the south side of the street. His granddaughter Martha married a rising politician, George Washington. An admission ticket is required to visit the garden. The house, office, and kitchen are now hotel guest accommodations.

Mary Stith, daughter of William Stith, president of the College of William and Mary from 1752 to 1755, owned the small structure that is known as the ■**Mary Stith House.** In her will of 1813, she left this lot, its buildings, and much of her estate to her "coloured people" in gratitude for past services. Today, visitors to this reconstructed building enjoy special interpretive programs and encounters with "People of the Past" who portray eighteenth-century citizens.

Next door is the **James Anderson House,** a site that served at various times as a residence and place of business for a tavern keeper, a milliner, a barber and perukemaker, and a chandler and soap boiler before Anderson purchased the property in 1770. Anderson lived at the corner of Francis and Botetourt Streets on the adjoining half lot. He probably purchased this property to accommodate his expanding business.

Behind the house is the ■**James Anderson Blacksmith Shop.** With the exception of the years 1781–1783, when he relocated the business to Richmond following his primary customer, the state government, Anderson operated a blacksmith and armorer's shop here from the late 1770s until he died in 1798. During the Revolutionary War, Anderson was

contracted by the Commonwealth of Virginia to do armorer's work, including cleaning and repairing muskets, swords, and bayonets and manufacturing nails, axes, tomahawks, and vehicle hardware.

This reconstructed shop is one of several buildings associated with the prosperous industrial site. Extensive archaeological excavations revealed the foundations of the forges and workshop, and the building was reconstructed in the mid-1980s using techniques common in the eighteenth century. Construction details were based on thorough field studies of surviving eighteenth-century structures that reflect the style typical of agricultural buildings of the period.

Inside the shop are tools and materials typical of a blacksmith's business in the colonial period. Coal-fired forges and hammers, anvils, files, saws, punches, chisels, and many other tools are used to shape iron and steel into useful articles. The smiths who work here today reproduce iron objects using technology that would have been familiar to James Anderson and his workmen. The shop's segmented appearance and coarse construction reflect the rapid growth of a purely industrial building in response to increased wartime demands for ironwork.

Next door, the **Brick House Tavern** was built as a rental property in the early 1760s. The building provided twelve residences with twelve separate entrances (six in front, six in the rear). Itinerant tradesmen and others with services or goods to sell would arrange for lodging here, advertise in the *Virginia Gazette,* and show their wares to customers in their rooms. If business seemed promising, they might settle down elsewhere in town; if not, they would move on. Over time, a surgeon, jeweler, watch repairer, milliner, wigmaker, and several tavern keepers, to name a few, called the Brick House Tavern home. Today, it is a hotel facility, as is the Brick House Tavern Shop behind it.

FROM BOTETOURT STREET TO THE CAPITOL

Tarpley's Store, a commercial establishment, is located on the south side of the street.

Brick House Tavern   *James Anderson House*

Merchant James Tarpley erected and operated his store on this lot after it was subdivided in 1759. Newspaper advertisements show that local residents considered this block "the most public part of the city" and "the most convenient spot . . . for trade." Later in the century, Alexander Purdie published a rival *Virginia Gazette* here. Purdie's newspaper bore the motto "Always for Liberty, and the Publick Good." He was appointed public printer just before the Revolution. Merchandise typical of that sold in the eighteenth century is available at Tarpley's Store.

Across the street two residences, the **Prentis House** and the **Russell House**, break up the otherwise commercial character of the block. An admission ticket is required to visit the charming garden behind the Prentis House.

The ■**Margaret Hunter Shop,** an original structure, typically presents its gable end to

the street. The brickwork is original except for a few patches. The blue-green glaze on some of the bricks resulted from their having been nearest to the heat while they were being fired in the kiln. The shop occupies a favorable spot on the busy "downtown" end of Duke of Gloucester Street. The sales area is in front, and there is a small counting room in the back.

The word "milliner" is believed to have derived from "Milaner," meaning a person who came from, or imported goods from, Milan, Italy. The colonial milliner was a shopkeeper who sold fashionable household goods. An important businesswoman, she imported cloth and made clothing and accessories, principally for women and children. A 1774 advertisement details the sorts of merchandise that Margaret Hunter stocked: "Jet necklaces and earrings, black love ribands, Sleeve Knots, Stuff Shoes for Ladies, Women's and children's riding habits, dressed and undressed Babies, toys, scotch snuff, and Busts of the late Lord Botetourt," a popular governor. Like some other shopkeepers in Williamsburg, Margaret Hunter lived above her store.

The ■**Golden Ball** was the address of James Craig, a jeweler and silversmith from London, who established his business at this location in 1765. Craig once made a pair of earrings for Patsy Custis, the stepdaughter of George Washington. In 1772, Craig added a watch-

■*James Anderson Blacksmith Shop*

■ *Mary Stith House*

Orlando Jones Office and House

Prentis House

Russell House

■ *Margaret Hunter Shop (Milliner)*

maker to his staff and began advertising his store as the "Golden Ball," a trademark commonly used by jewelers and goldsmiths. Craig lived and worked on these premises with his family of five and one slave until he died in the early 1790s.

The original building on this site was built in 1724 and survived until 1907. A photograph, archaeological excavations of the foundations, and the recollections of former residents guided the reconstruction. Today, skilled silversmiths create beautiful objects by hand on the west side of the Golden Ball, and silver hollowware and gold and silver jewelry are sold on the east side. (An admission ticket is not required to enter the store on the east side of the Golden Ball.)

Next door, the double brick structure divided into the **Unicorn's Horn and John Carter's Store** was built in 1765 by two brothers. Dr. James Carter used the west portion as an apothecary shop under the distinctive sign of the unicorn's horn. His brother John ran a

general store in the building's eastern half.

Across the street is ■**Wetherburn's Tavern,** one of the most important of the town's surviving buildings because it has been so thoroughly documented—architecturally as a carefully studied original building, archaeologically through extensive excavations, and historically by surviving deeds, accounts, and a room-by-room inventory taken after the death of Henry Wetherburn, its long-time owner-operator, in 1760.

Charlton House

■ *Wetherburn's Tavern*

■ *Golden Ball*
(Jeweler and Engraver)

Unicorn's Horn and
John Carter's Store

A colonial tavern was quite different from its modern namesake. In addition to serving liquor and ale, it also offered lodging for travelers, meals, and a place for socializing and entertaining. Cards, dice, and conversation were as important as food and drink. Wetherburn's "great room," which measures twenty-five feet square and occupies most of the west end of the first floor, occasionally served as an informal town hall in which scientific lectures, political gatherings, and balls were held.

A large-scale enterprise, Wetherburn's depended on the enslaved to cook, serve, clean, tend the garden, and groom customers' horses. Henry Wetherburn owned twelve slaves, including seven women (one with a young daughter), an adult man, and three boys. They would have lived in the attics over the kitchen and stable.

After Wetherburn's death in 1760, a long and detailed inventory of his estate listed the contents of the building room by room. It has been a principal guide in refurnishing the restored tavern. Additional information came from the painstaking excavations made by Colonial Williamsburg archaeologists, who recovered more than two hundred thousand fragments of pottery, glass, and metal objects from the site.

The outbuildings, vegetable garden, and yard form one of the most thoroughly researched dependency areas in Williamsburg. The dairy survives with its original framing. The other outbuildings, including the kitchen,

in which there is a huge fireplace, were reconstructed on their eighteenth-century locations, which were revealed by modern archaeological excavations.

In 1770, wigmaker Edward Charlton owned the neighboring **Charlton House**. Charlton kept an account book that details his wigmaking activities between 1769 and 1774. It shows that his customers included burgesses—such as Thomas Jefferson, Patrick Henry, and Colonel Lewis Burwell of Kingsmill plantation—and town residents—George Wythe, Thomas Everard, Peyton Randolph,

and Peter Pelham to name a few—as well as local tavern keepers, merchants, and tradesmen. In addition to charges for wigs (brown dress bob wigs at two pounds, three shillings, were popular), shaving, and hair dressing, Charlton also sold pairs of curls to the wives and daughters of his customers.

Williamsburg's working version of a wig

Tarpley's Store

shop, the ▪King's Arms Barber Shop, has been reconstructed. The barber pole is based on one in an eighteenth-century print by English artist William Hogarth. In colonial days, a wigmaker was also known as a peruke-maker, a name derived from the French word "perruque," or "wig."

Jane Vobe, one of Williamsburg's most successful tavern keepers, ran the **King's Arms Tavern.** In 1772, she announced her location as "opposite the Raleigh, at the Sign of the King's Arms," a name that she changed to the Eagle Tavern after the Revolution.

During the war, when Mrs. Vobe supplied food and drink to American troops, Baron von Steuben ran up a bill of nearly three hundred Spanish dollars for lodging, meals, and beverages. The King's Arms offers traditional southern dishes served in an atmosphere reminiscent of colonial days.

The reconstructed **Alexander Purdie House** serves as the east wing of the King's Arms Tavern. In 1774, the Scottish-born Purdie founded the third of three Williamsburg newspapers named the *Virginia Gazette*. All three papers competed for readers as the Revolution drew near.

The **John Coke Office** next door was named for an early nineteenth-century keeper of the Raleigh Tavern.

Across the street is the ▪**Raleigh Tavern,** the foremost of Williamsburg's taverns in the eighteenth century. Established about 1717, the Raleigh grew in size and reputation through the years. Letters, diaries, newspaper advertisements, and other records indicate that the Raleigh was one of the most important taverns in colonial Virginia. It served as a center for social, commercial, and political gatherings, small private and large public dinners, lectures and exhibits, and auctions of merchandise, property, and the enslaved.

During "Publick Times," when the courts were in session, the Raleigh hummed with activity. Gentlemen and ladies attended elegant balls in its popular Apollo Room. Planters and merchants gathered at its bar. Sturdy tavern tables were scarred by dice boxes; tobacco smoke from long clay pipes filled the air. Good fellowship and business deals were sealed by a toast of Madeira or by a pint of ale drunk from a pewter tankard.

Although he generally stayed elsewhere, George Washington often noted in his diary that he "dined at the Raleigh." After one evening of revelry in 1763, twenty-year-old Thomas Jefferson, then reading law under the learned George Wythe's supervision, complained in a letter to a friend: "Last night as merry as agreeable company and dancing with Belinda in the Apollo could make me, I never could have thought the succeeding Sun would have seen me so wretched."

Public receptions were common. In 1775, Peyton Randolph was entertained at the Raleigh when he returned from serving as the president of the first Continental Congress, which met in Philadelphia. The following year,

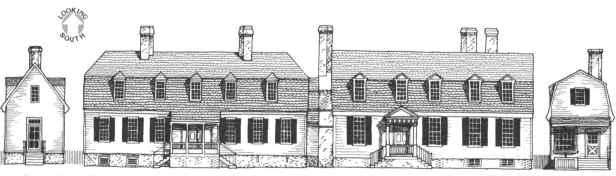

John Coke Office   Alexander Purdie House   King's Arms Tavern   ▪King's Arms Barber Shop (Wigmaker)

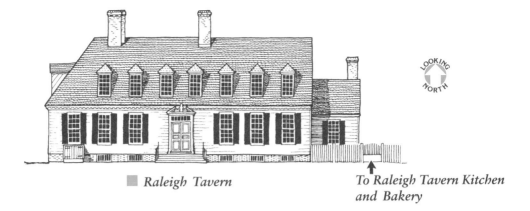

Raleigh Tavern

↑ To Raleigh Tavern Kitchen and Bakery

Virginia troops in Williamsburg gave a farewell dinner in honor of their esteemed commander, Patrick Henry. After the Treaty of Paris ending the Revolution was proclaimed in the city, the citizens of the new republic concluded their triumphal parade with a celebration at the Raleigh Tavern. General Lafayette was welcomed on his return to Williamsburg in 1824 by a banquet in the Apollo Room.

Becoming Americans
Our Struggle to Be Both Free and Equal

THE INSTITUTION OF SLAVERY

Slavery created great divisions in eighteenth-century Virginia because it fostered the development of a social structure based on race.

The rise of the plantation system and the dwindling supply of white servants led to the large-scale importation of slaves. Europeans forced the migration of 11.5 million Africans between the sixteenth and nineteenth centuries. Approximately six hundred thousand were brought into British North America.

A series of laws formalized Virginia's system of slavery. In the seventeenth century, when there were few Africans in the colony, the legislators worked to define who was a slave and to make slavery permanent and hereditary. When Virginia's slave population increased after 1700, colonial leaders enacted laws to restrict the movement of slaves, set punishments for legal infractions, and reinforced a slaveholder's right to his property. As a result, the cultural, religious, and social differences between blacks and whites became sharper in the eighteenth century.

Although Africans could not alter formal institutions, individual slaves were able to shape personal relationships with whites. They also participated in a local, increasingly cash-based trading economy. Blacks and whites influenced one another's culture as well. Rather than being a process that blacks or whites consciously pursued, cultural sharing was the inevitable result of their interaction in all areas of their lives.

Alexander Craig House   *Scrivener Store*

The tavern's location, its convenient meeting rooms, and (one suspects) its proprietors' sympathy for the colonists' cause made it a center of political activities in the colonial capital during the 1760s and 1770s. In 1769, when Governor Botetourt dissolved the General Assembly because of its protest against the Townshend Acts, many indignant burgesses reconvened at the tavern to draw up a boycott of British goods. Five years later, the Assembly again being dissolved, other non-importation measures were agreed upon at the Raleigh after the shocking news reached Virginia that Great Britain had ordered the port of Boston closed. The "late representatives of the people" issued the call for delegates from all the colonies to meet in the first Continental Congress.

The Raleigh Tavern burned in 1859. Architects who reconstructed the building were aided by two drawings made in 1848, by insurance policies, and by archaeological excavations that revealed most of the original foundations of the tavern and many colonial artifacts. Inventories of the possessions of its eighteenth-century proprietors guided the refurnishing of the Raleigh. After the death of

Anthony Hay in 1770, for example, the inventory listed most articles in the tavern.

The gentlemen of colonial Virginia and their ladies would find little changed if they returned to dance their minuets again. Charter members of the Phi Beta Kappa Society, founded in Williamsburg in 1776, could once more meet in the Apollo Room. The Raleigh's pervasive spirit of hospitality is well expressed in the motto gilded over the Apollo Room mantel: *Hilaritas Sapientiae et Bonae Vitae Proles*—"Jollity, the offspring of wisdom and good living."

Today visitors can purchase bread, cookies, and other baked products at the **Raleigh Tavern Bakery** in the **Raleigh Tavern Kitchen.** (An admission ticket is not required

The Apollo Room

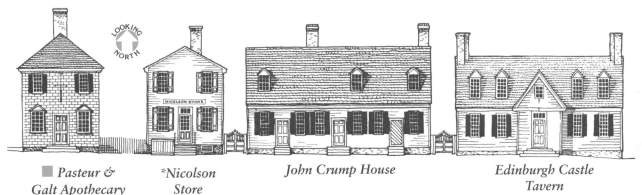

■ *Pasteur & Galt Apothecary Shop*   **Nicolson Store*   *John Crump House*   *Edinburgh Castle Tavern*

to enter the Raleigh Tavern Bakery.)

Commercial establishments lined nearly all the rest of Duke of Gloucester Street from the Raleigh to the Capitol. The **Alexander Craig House, Scrivener Store, Nicolson Store,** and **John Crump House** were, respectively, a saddle and harness shop, grocery store, general store, and residence.

At mid-century, **Edinburgh Castle Tavern** and **Shields Tavern** competed for the trade of the traveling public. In the early 1740s, James Shields took over the tavern that his Huguenot father-in-law, John Marot, had operated several decades earlier. Although located close to the Capitol, Shields Tavern attracted lower gentry and successful middling customers. Present-day visitors dine in a setting that depicts tavern keeping during the second quarter of the eighteenth century.

At the ■**Pasteur & Galt Apothecary Shop,** Dr. William Pasteur and Dr. John Galt had a partnership from 1775 to 1778. Both of these apothecary-surgeons apprenticed in Williamsburg and studied at Saint Thomas's Hospital in London. Today, the shop displays copies of Dr. Galt's certificates in surgery and anatomy, midwifery, and general medicine from London. Antique English and Dutch jars, pharmaceutical equipment, a traveling medical kit, and surgical tools, some original to the site, are also on display.

The shop also features reproduction splints for broken bones and dental tools for clean-

Shields Tavern

ing and extracting teeth. Period medications such as tincture of Peruvian bark for intermittent fever, chalk troches for heartburn, and licorce root for sore throat are also featured, as are other preparations containing active ingredients used in medicine today.

The building nearest the Capitol on the south side of Duke of Gloucester Street is the **Palmer House,** which bears the name of John Palmer, lawyer and bursar of the college of William and Mary. Palmer built his house on the site of an old store. During the Civil War, the dwelling served as a military headquarters, first for Confederate General Joseph Johnston and then for General George B. McClellan, the commander of the Union forces. The "put-log" holes in the brickwork were left when the masons who built the

Palmer House removed their scaffolding.

Merchants met in the open area that terminates Duke of Gloucester Street just before the Capitol wall to set prices of tobacco and other agricultural products and to trade in commercial paper. The Exchange functioned much like a modern commodities market, dealing in futures and risk. After the capital moved to Richmond in 1780, the Exchange—like Williamsburg as a whole—decreased in importance.

In October 1765, the Exchange was the scene of a near-riot when Colonel George Mercer, distributor of stamps for Virginia, arrived in Williamsburg from London prepared to distribute stamped paper when the hated Stamp Act went into effect on November 1. A large group of merchants and plant-

MEET . . . ROBERT NICOLSON

"We intend to make use of a House in the City of Williamsburgh . . . as a place of Public Worship of God according to the Practise of Protestant Dissenters of the Presbyterian denomination." So stated Robert Nicolson of Williamsburg and sixteen other men in a petition to a local court in 1765. Notifying the court enabled them to worship legally outside the Church of England in Virginia.

Before he became a dissenter, Nicolson and his wife, Mary, probably walked to Bruton Parish Church to worship on Sundays. They paid taxes that the vestry levied to meet church expenses, which included the minister's salary and support for the poor. If Robert and Mary missed too many services, Anglican churchwardens could take them to court, a good reason to attend church regularly.

Although he had become a Presbyterian, Robert Nicolson still was obliged to pay taxes to support Bruton Parish Church. Nicolson's decision to proclaim himself a dissenter made him one of a growing number of Virginians who wanted the freedom to worship as they chose.

A tailor by trade, Nicolson also took in lodgers and kept a store. Over time he acquired a lot in town, thirty-five acres in the country, and two slaves, but Nicolson never rose above the middling rank of Williamsburg society.

In 1776, the General Assembly suspended the requirement that dissenters pay parish taxes. The legislature passed the Virginia Statute for Religious Freedom ten years later.

ers surrounded Mercer as he attempted to reach Governor Fauquier, who was waiting with other high-ranking government officials on the porch of a nearby coffeehouse. The crowd demanded to know if Mercer intended to resign. He replied that he would answer them on November 1, after he had met with the governor.

*Palmer House

The angry men followed Mercer to the coffeehouse, where he joined Fauquier. The crowd demanded an answer before the act went into effect and began to storm the porch. Fauquier and other officials stepped forward to shield Mercer. The forward push stopped. Mercer reluctantly agreed to give an answer before November 1, and the governor escorted him to the Palace. Mercer resigned the next day.

The House of Burgesses had passed protest resolves introduced by Patrick Henry and supported by his famous "Caesar–Brutus" speech in May 1765. Virginians continued to argue strongly that the Stamp Act was an abridgement of their traditional British liberties because a legislature (Parliament) in which they were not represented had enacted it.

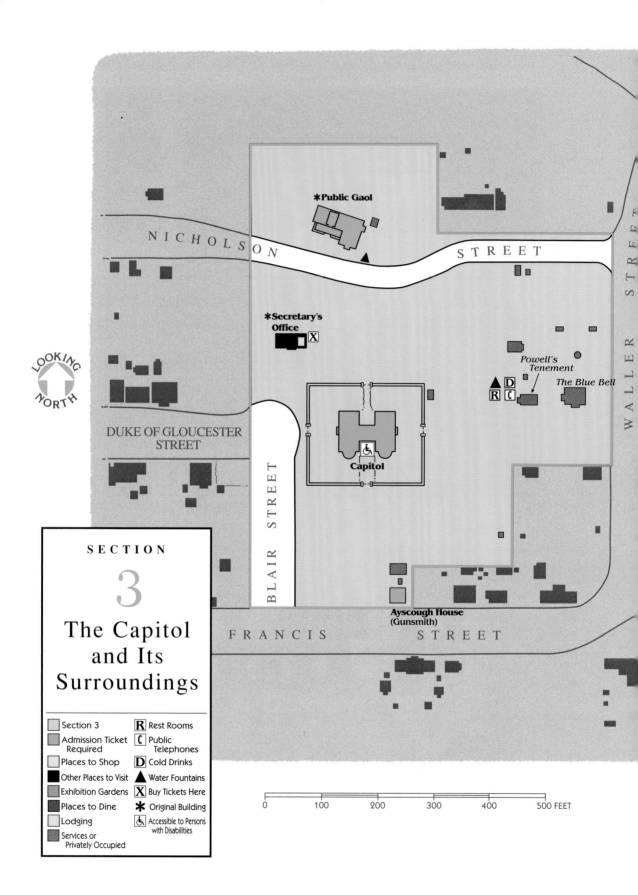

*Public Gaol

NICHOLSON STREET

*Secretary's Office X

Powell's Tenement

The Blue Bell

▲ D
R C

Capitol

DUKE OF GLOUCESTER STREET

BLAIR STREET

WALLER STREET

FRANCIS STREET

Ayscough House
(Gunsmith)

SECTION

3

The Capitol and Its Surroundings

☐ Section 3	R Rest Rooms
☐ Admission Ticket Required	C Public Telephones
☐ Places to Shop	D Cold Drinks
■ Other Places to Visit	▲ Water Fountains
☐ Exhibition Gardens	X Buy Tickets Here
☐ Places to Dine	✱ Original Building
☐ Lodging	♿ Accessible to Persons with Disabilities
☐ Services or Privately Occupied	

0   100   200   300   400   500 FEET

LOOKING NORTH

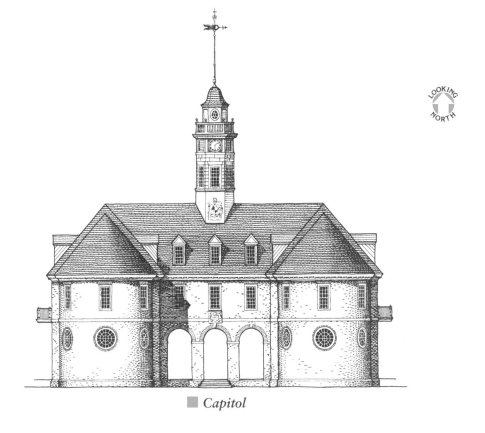

■ *Capitol*

THE CAPITOL AND ITS SURROUNDINGS

An asterisk (*) indicates that a building is an original eighteenth- or nineteenth-century structure. A ■ *indicates that you need an admission ticket to see an attraction.*

For eighty years, Williamsburg was the political center of Virginia, one of England's largest, wealthiest, and most populous colonies. Here laws and justice were made and administered on behalf of all colonial Virginians. The first and second Capitol buildings, the Public Gaol, and the Secretary's Office were visible reminders that these buildings and the activities that went on inside them gave Williamsburg a political importance second to that of no other colonial capital.

At the Capitol, the General Assembly debated and framed legislation and the courts dispensed justice. Most of the important records of the colony—legal documents of every kind—were kept in a separate building, the Secretary's Office. Nearby, at the Public Gaol, Virginians accused of felonies or imprisoned for debts languished until their cases could be heard in court.

Spring and fall sessions of the General Court, summer and winter sessions of the criminal court, and sessions of the General Assembly, which were convened by the governor, provided the formal occasions that brought the Capitol area to life. Other, more informal activities animated the scene year-round because the bureaucratic machinery that kept the wheels of government turning operated continuously.

The H-shaped plan of the Capitol is an early example of an architectural design successfully devised for a specific purpose. It also reflects the makeup of Virginia's colonial government.

Representative government in Virginia began at Jamestown in 1619. As the General Assembly evolved, it comprised the Council and the House of Burgesses, each of which met separately.

The east wing of the Capitol contained the House of Burgesses on the first floor and committee rooms for the burgesses on the second. The House of Burgesses, the lower house of the legislature, consisted of two members elected by the landowners of each county and one member each from Jamestown, Williamsburg, Norfolk, and the College of William and Mary.

The west wing housed the General Court-

room on the first floor and the Council Chamber on the second. The Council, made up of twelve leading colonists appointed for life by the king, constituted the upper house of the legislature. The councillors also assisted the governor by acting as a council of state. In its legislative capacity, the Council met in the elegant Council Chamber. Each wing had its own staircase.

The General Assembly convened periodically in the Capitol to act on a wide range of legislation. In the course of a session, which could have lasted a few days or several weeks, the upper and lower houses might have considered the petition of a veteran for public assistance or frontier settlers asking that a new county or church parish be formed. The legislators could divide large counties into smaller ones or move a county's courthouse to a more central location. They considered aiding other colonies in wartime and at the same time es-

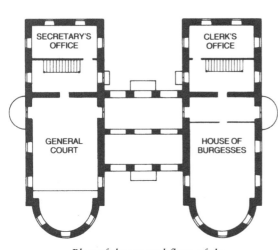

Plan of the ground floor of the reconstructed Capitol

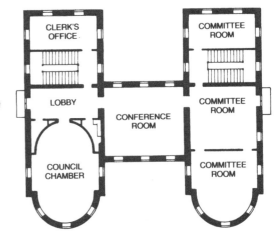

Plan of the upper floor of the reconstructed Capitol

tablished Virginia's own frontier defenses. They settled public claims and levied taxes to pay for them. And, as the imperial crisis of the 1760s and 1770s worsened, they spent more and more time debating remonstrations to submit to King George III and Parliament.

If the two houses deadlocked in trying to pass a bill already accepted by one or the other, representatives from the Council and the burgesses met jointly in the second-floor chamber located over the piazza. In effect, this conference room formed a bridge between the two buildings. The architecture of the Capitol thus aided the process of mediation between the two houses. Morning prayers were also held in the conference room.

The foundations of the original building were laid in 1701. Impatient with meeting at the College of William and Mary, Virginia's lawmakers moved into the new Capitol in 1704, a year before its completion.

As a precaution against fire, Williamsburg's first Capitol was designed without chimneys, and the use of fire, candles, or tobacco was strictly prohibited. In time, such safeguards were sacrificed to necessity and convenience. A secretary complained, for example, that his records were "exposed by the Damps." Two chimneys were therefore added in 1723. Despite precautions, however, fire gutted the building on January 30, 1747, leaving "the naked Brick Walls only . . . standing."

With the encouragement of Governor William Gooch, a second Capitol, completed in 1753, was built. It incorporated the surviving walls of its predecessor but differed in appearance. After the removal of Virginia's government to Richmond in 1780, the second building fell into disrepair, and in 1832, it, too, was destroyed by fire.

Before reconstruction could be undertaken, Colonial Williamsburg faced a dilemma: should the first or second building rise again on the old foundations? The second Capitol was of greater historic interest, since it wit-

nessed the events of the years before the Revolution, but the first Capitol could lay claim to greater architectural distinction. Its rounded ends, for instance, were unique. Moreover, long searching of the architectural evidence disclosed voluminous information about the earlier building, whereas few records were available for the later one. As a result, the first Capitol was reconstructed.

Two courts met regularly in the Capitol. The General Court, the highest court of the colony, convened in April and October to hear both civil and criminal cases. The governor and the twelve members of the Council served as the justices of the General Court. After 1710, the Court of Oyer and Terminer (meaning "to hear and decide"), presided over by the councillors alone, heard criminal cases at sessions in June and December.

Punishment for serious crimes was harsh in the eighteenth century, and the death penalty was the rule for offenses such as arson, horse stealing, forgery, burglary—and piracy. First offenders or criminals with particularly moving pleas might, however, receive clemency. In 1727, convicted teenage pirate John Vidal, who pitifully protested that he "never intended to go a-pirating" and "with

The Great Union flag (left) *became the national standard of Great Britain and her colonies in 1606. It flies today over the Capitol. The Grand Union flag* (right) *became the first American flag to fly in Williamsburg on May 15, 1776.*

The reproduction Speaker's chair in the House of Burgesses is based on the original probably made by a Williamsburg cabinetmaker for the first Capitol about 1735. Moved to Richmond with the state's possessions in 1780, the original was returned to Williamsburg through the courtesy of the Virginia legislature. It is on dislay at the DeWitt Wallace Decorative Arts Museum.

a weeping heart" begged for mercy, received His Majesty's most gracious pardon.

Ceremony and formality characterized the proceedings of these legislative and judicial bodies and the behavior of their members. When a new governor arrived, he was customarily met by a delegation and conveyed directly to the Capitol to be sworn to the king's commission. The opening ceremony of the General Assembly was patterned after the opening of Parliament. Governor Botetourt rode down Duke of Gloucester Street to the Capitol in a gilded state coach drawn by six matching gray horses. Burgesses assembled in the Council Chamber, took their oaths of office in the presence of the Council, and returned to the House to elect a Speaker. Upon the governor's formal approval of the Speaker's election, the mace of the House, which had been placed under the table, was returned to the table top and the burgesses

proceeded with their legislative business.

Parliamentary privilege exercised by the English Parliament extended to the House of Burgesses to protect the House and its members against slander. In 1723, burgess Mathew Kemp complained that attorney William Hopkins had uttered "several rude Contemptious and undecent Expressions" about Kemp's conduct in the House. The burgesses found Hopkins guilty of contempt and ordered him to kneel, "acknowlege his Offence, and ask pardon of this House and Mr. Kemp." Hopkins refused. The burgesses next ordered that Hopkins, wearing a sign that proclaimed his offenses, be led from the Capitol to the college and back again. Then he was to be imprisoned. Upon hearing this, a chastened Hopkins knelt, expressed sorrow, and prayed mercy of the House, which fined and then discharged him.

Some of the colony's most powerful officials had offices in the Capitol. The secretary, usually a member of the Council, was appointed by the king. His office issued all land patents and most other documents, including naturalization papers and passports, that required the seal of the colony.

The auditor examined all colonial revenue accounts and forwarded them to Treasury officials in London. The receiver general took in and disbursed the colony's "royal revenues." The attorney general also had an office in the Capitol. He gave legal advice to the governor and his Council, prosecuted criminal cases before the General Court, and, after 1720, served as the sole judge of the Vice Admiralty Court. Because he was the king's attorney, the attorney general was never a councillor.

A memorable historical event occurred at the Capitol on May 15, 1776, when Virginia's legislators pledged their lives and fortunes by taking the daring step of declaring their full freedom from England. The burgesses adopted a resolution for American independence without a dissenting vote.

ℬecoming ℭAmericans
Our Struggle to Be Both Free and Equal

CHOOSING REVOLUTION

Colonial Williamsburg programs trace the development of the new nation by exploring the complex decision every Virginian faced: whether to remain loyal to the British Crown or to separate from the mother country.

When Virginia's political leaders began to protest imperial policies in the early 1760s, none imagined a separate nation. Yet by the middle of the next decade, issues and choices had transformed traditional ideals of British liberty into a revolutionary, American political philosophy based on freedom, liberty, and popular sovereignty that Americans were ready to defend with arms.

Two contending groups were central to the conflict between Virginia and Great Britain. After the Seven Years' War, the British ministry, backed by Parliament, sought active management of the vast empire that Britain had acquired. Their policies often came into conflict with Virginia's powerful political leaders, who were determined to protect their prerogative to draft legislation for the colony.

Political leaders in Virginia were generally united on the basic issues, but they divided over the best course to follow. The elder statesmen tended to be conservative. They counseled moderation. The younger, more aggressive leadership urged forceful and direct protests against British policies that threatened property rights. To protest effectively, they needed the support of the yeomanry. Increasingly diverse in ethnicity and religion, the yeomanry responded to the gentry leadership's appeal to property rights by becoming active politically. The gentry's promotion of property ownership as almost a sacred right protected the practice of slavery, however.

Going to war against Great Britain was a bold—some said a suicidal—act. Once war was declared, whites of all social ranks, free blacks, the enslaved, and Native Americans considered both ideology and self-interest as they chose, or did not choose, revolution. Taking one side or the other required sacrifice. A significant number sat on the fence as long as possible. Some switched sides. Dependent family members usually accepted the choice of the head of the household and shared in the consequences, although sons or slaves occasionally made opposite choices.

Out of the war came American principles of nation building, among them the conflicting ideals of individual liberty and the public good. Through government channels established by the U. S. Constitution, Americans today continue to struggle to achieve a balance between these two ideals and to extend them to groups that have not enjoyed them. Americans ceaselessly reexamine how to attain liberty, freedom, and equality, the ideals for which the American Revolution was fought.

Secretary's Office

On June 7, 1776, Richard Henry Lee, one of Virginia's delegates, acting on this resolution, introduced a motion for independence on the floor of the Continental Congress at Philadelphia. His proposal led directly to the Declaration of Independence, drafted largely by Thomas Jefferson, who had stood at the half-open door of the House of Burgesses in Williamsburg eleven years before to hear Patrick Henry thunder his defiance of Parliament and king.

Patrick Henry, the first governor of the Commonwealth of Virginia

Before a separate Secretary's Office was built, the most important public papers of the colony were stored in an office next to the General Courtroom. There, the chief clerk and his deputy oversaw a vast domain of records in the form of bound volumes and of endless files of loose papers tied up in red tape that had been used by bureaucrats to secure legal and official documents since the seventeenth century. Here, generations of clerk-apprentices scribbled away, learning their trade.

When the Capitol burned in 1747, officials fortunately were able to save a number of documents that included land office records, executive papers of the clerk of the Council, and the files of the clerk of the House of Burgesses. Afterward, it took nearly a year to sort them all out.

After the fire, the burgesses and Council agreed in principle on the necessity of building a separate **Secretary's Office.** But while the burgesses' approval was delayed by a debate about whether to move the capital farther inland, the Council acted decisively. It contracted for and oversaw the erection of a repository for the public records. The building was completed at a cost of £367 19s. 6d., paid for out of royal revenues, by December 1748.

The new Secretary's Office was clearly designed to avoid fire at all costs. There was neither basement nor attic, the original floor was paved with stones, and the interior walls and window jambs were plastered-over brick. Little wood was used in the construction. There were, however, four fireplaces in the three-room structure to provide heat in winter and drive off the damp and mold in summer. Tidewater humidity can be as destructive as fire to paper and leather.

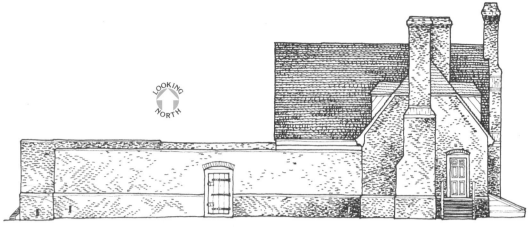

■ *Public Gaol*

It would be hard to overestimate the potential influence in the colony of the office of the secretary. Perhaps the most significant of his privileges was the power to appoint the clerks of all the county courts in Virginia. To supply a trained cadre of these young men, five to seven apprentice clerks were always at work in the secretary's office. Sent there at their family's expense to serve an apprenticeship of seven years, they then waited their turn to be named to the next vacant clerkship. This system produced a body of clerks who had been trained to the same standards.

After the capital and its records moved to Richmond in 1780, the Secretary's Office was occupied for a time by the Court of Admiralty under Justice Benjamin Waller. When the Capitol became a private grammar school, the Secretary's Office was refitted as a home for the headmaster. Today, it houses exhibitions on the Revolution and a gift shop where you can purchase books, gift items, and admission tickets.

The ■**Public Gaol** (pronounced "jail"), just north of the Capitol on Nicholson Street, affords today grim evidence of crime and punishment in colonial America.

Accused offenders were imprisoned in the Gaol only until their cases came to trial in the Capitol before either the General Court or the Court of Oyer and Terminer, the criminal court. Insolvent debtors awaiting relief or mercy were occasionally held in the Gaol.

Their numbers were greatly reduced by a 1772 act that made creditors wholly responsible for their debtors' maintenance and tripled the fees charged for their board. Runaway slaves were detained at the Gaol until their masters claimed them and paid their expenses.

The Gaol at times housed insane persons and military prisoners. Until the Public Hospital opened in 1773, some mentally ill individuals were occasionally confined in the Gaol. In the early years of the Revolution, the Gaol was crowded with captured British redcoats, tory sympathizers, and accused traitors, deserters, and spies. Henry Hamilton, the British governor of the Northwest Territory, widely known as the "Hair Buyer" because he allegedly paid his Indian allies for American scalps, was detained in the Public Gaol in 1779–1780.

Prison conditions in colonial days would be judged both crude and cruel by modern standards. The use of leg irons, handcuffs, and chains seems inhumane. Even if the night was bitterly cold, prisoners of every description bedded down with only a thin blanket. A diet of "salt beef damaged, and Indian meal" could not have been very appetizing. Yet prisoners were allowed to converse and walk about the exercise yard during the day, use the crude sanitary arrangements (the "thrones" in each cell), and were given "physick," or medicine, when ill. Prisoners with money or

MEET . . . PETER PELHAM

Peter Pelham was a man of much ability. Born in England in 1721, Pelham came to America in 1726 with his father. They settled in Boston, where Pelham studied music and became organist at Trinity Church. Pelham became artist John Singleton Copley's stepbrother when his father married Copley's widowed mother.

Pelham moved to Williamsburg about 1750. In 1755, he not only set up the new organ ordered for Bruton Parish Church but was "unanimously appointed and chosen organist." As a member of the Williamsburg Lodge of Masons, Pelham played the organ at the funeral of fellow Mason and *Virginia Gazette* publisher William Rind. Pelham taught young ladies to play the harpsichord and spinet, and he served as musical director when *The Beggar's Opera* was first performed in Williamsburg.

Pelham and his wife, Ann, had fourteen children, some of whom died in infancy. Like many artists then and now, Pelham's musical talents did not always generate enough income to maintain his large family. He supplemented his income by serving as clerk to Governors Fauquier and Botetourt and as keeper of the Public Gaol. Until he left Williamsburg in 1802, "the modern Orpheus—the inimitable Pelham" continued as church organist, and he also gave weekly concerts to the delight of many townsfolk.

accommodating friends could purchase food and liquor from one of the taverns nearby or obtain clothing and blankets to supplement those issued at the Gaol.

Legislation that was passed in 1701 called for the construction of a "substantial Brick Prison" twenty by thirty feet. The act further provided for an adjoining walled exercise yard. Debtors' cells were added in 1711, and quarters for the gaoler were built in 1722. In its present form, the Public Gaol has three rooms on the first floor—a hall and chamber for the gaoler and his family and a cell at the rear for debtors— and "chambers" in the attic for the gaoler's use and the confinement of petty offenders.

The gaolkeepers, who often served as custodians of the Capitol, were appointed by the governor. Gaolers had a rough and dangerous job for which they were paid a modest salary. The first keeper, John Redwood, received thirty pounds annually. This amount was supplemented by prisoners' fees and eventually increased by the General Assembly.

The Gaol served colony and commonwealth until 1780. A portion of the original building continued to be used by the city of Williamsburg as its jail until 1910. Part of the brickwork of the Gaol's massive walls is original. Shackles unearthed in the course of the building's restoration are evidence of the bleak life of a colonial criminal.

LOOKING NORTH

■ Ayscough House (Gunsmith)

The ■**Ayscough House** was the site of one of many establishments that grew up around the Capitol. Artisans, retailers, and tavern keepers located near the Capitol enjoyed the business of the councillors, burgesses, attorneys, and others who came to participate in court cases or deliberate legislation. Proximity to the Capitol did not ensure success, however. Christopher Ayscough, a former gardener, and his wife, Anne, who had been the head cook for Lieutenant Governor Francis Fauquier at the Palace, purchased the Ayscough House and established a tavern there in 1768. The funds probably came from a bequest of £250 that Governor Fauquier left Anne "in recompense of her great fidelity and attention to me in all my illnesses and of the great Economy with which she conducted the Expenses of my Kitchen during my residence at Williamsburg."

The Ayscoughs' tavern-keeping venture proved to be short lived, however. Within two years, Christopher Ayscough, deeply in debt, offered to sell his dwelling along with furnishings, Madeira wine, slaves, and horses. Ayscough then became the doorkeeper at the Capitol, but in 1771, he was discharged for drunkenness. Today, gunsmiths at the Ayscough House use the tools and methods of their predecessors to make rifles, fowling pieces, and pistols like those crafted in colonial Virginia.

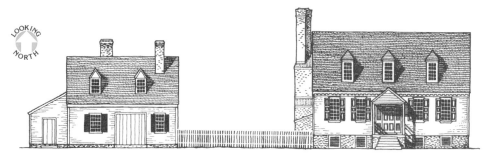

Powell's Tenement   *The Blue Bell*

In 1703, John Redwood, keeper of the Public Gaol, obtained a lot east of the Capitol, where he operated an ordinary. At various times in the eighteenth century, **The Blue Bell** housed a tavern, a lodging house, a store, a gunsmith's shop, and a tenement. After being informed in 1771 that his Williamsburg property, including The Blue Bell, was in "bad repair always rented to bad tenants, always nasty and few rents paid," absentee owner William Lee of London tried to sell the tavern but failed to find a buyer.

Wheelwright and riding chair maker Peter Powell rented a shop on the site of **Powell's Tenement** from 1755 to about 1770. In 1766, Powell advertised for an assistant, a blacksmith "who understands doing riding chair work." Later, in 1779, Powell's Tenement was occupied by the keeper of the Public Gaol.

The reconstructed building now houses the heating plant for the Capitol. **Powell's Kitchen** is behind.

In 1934, the year the reconstructed Capitol opened, John D. Rockefeller, Jr., addressed a commemorative session of the Virginia General Assembly. This was the first of many times that the Virginia legislature met in the Capitol at Williamsburg.

MEET . . . THOMAS WALKER

On March 6, 1750, Dr. Thomas Walker and five companions set out on a journey from Albemarle County. They traveled beyond the southwesternmost settlement in Virginia and through the Cumberland Gap into Kentucky before returning more than four months later. Dr. Walker and his colleagues were not the first whites to reach Kentucky, but, unlike earlier explorers, Walker kept careful notes of where he went and what he saw because the trip was more than an exciting adventure. As the general agent of the Loyal Land Company, Walker was expected to locate the best possible 800,000 acres granted to the company in July 1749.

Thomas Walker was born into a prominent family in King and Queen County in 1715. He moved to Williamsburg to live with his sister Mary and her husband, Dr. George Gilmer, as a teenager. Walker studied medicine in the colonial capital and then established a practice in Fredericksburg. Dr. Walker married Mildred, the widow of Nicholas Meriwether, in 1741. Managing his wife's dower lands at the foot of the Blue Ridge Mountains led to a new career for Walker, who began a long association with men such as Peter Jefferson and Joshua Fry, who saw Virginia's and their own futures tied to western expansion. Walker devoted his considerable skills to merging the interests of the Loyal Land Company, which he helped to create, with his own until his death.

Elected a burgess in 1752, Walker served regularly until 1775. Putting his knowledge of the West to good use, he lobbied effectively to protect the company from rivals. Walker entertained Indian delegations on their way to Williamsburg at his Albemarle home, and the trust he gained among them earned him successive appointments as a chief Indian negotiator. In that position, he was as attentive to Loyal Land Company interests as he was to Virginia's.

When Thomas Walker died in 1794, the Loyal Land Company had sold more than 200,000 acres in more than 900 tracts. What once had been Virginia's southwest frontier had become home to 38,000 settlers. And Kentucky was a new state in a new, westward-looking nation.

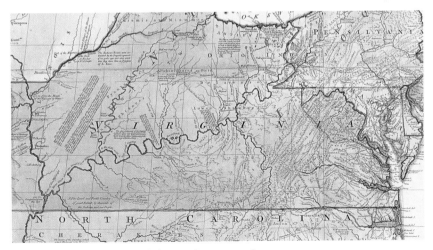

In 1755, Virginia was much larger than it is today.

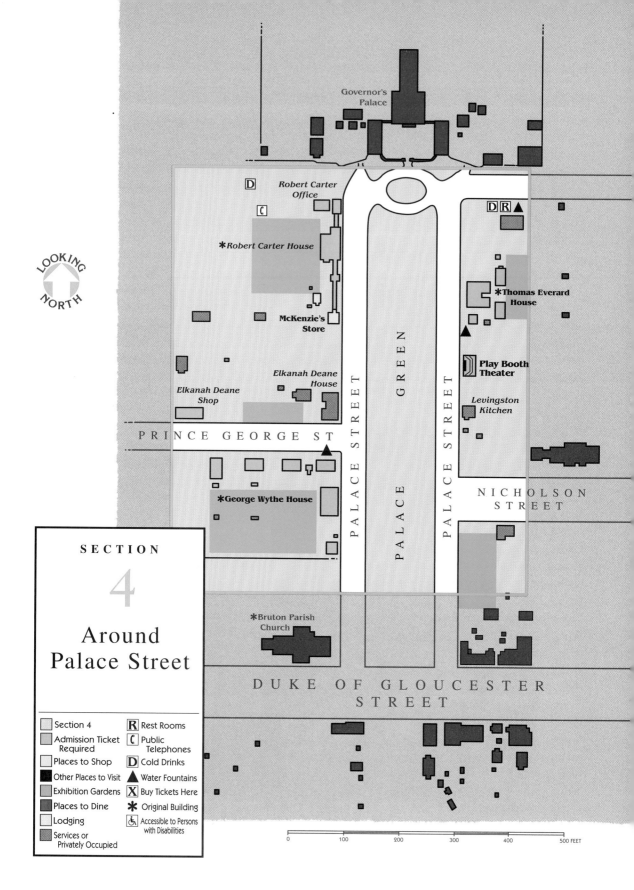

LOOKING NORTH

Governor's Palace

D Robert Carter Office

C

*Robert Carter House

McKenzie's Store

Elkanah Deane House

Elkanah Deane Shop

PRINCE GEORGE ST

PALACE STREET

PALACE GREEN

PALACE STREET

D R ▲

*Thomas Everard House

Play Booth Theater

Levingston Kitchen

NICHOLSON STREET

*George Wythe House

*Bruton Parish Church

DUKE OF GLOUCESTER STREET

SECTION

4

Around Palace Street

Section 4
Admission Ticket Required
Places to Shop
Other Places to Visit
Exhibition Gardens
Places to Dine
Lodging
Services or Privately Occupied

R Rest Rooms
C Public Telephones
D Cold Drinks
▲ Water Fountains
X Buy Tickets Here
* Original Building
♿ Accessible to Persons with Disabilities

0   100   200   300   400   500 FEET

AROUND PALACE STREET

An asterisk (*) indicates that a building is an original eighteenth- or nineteenth-century structure. A ■ indicates that you need an admission ticket to see an attraction.

When eighteenth-century visitors turned north from Duke of Gloucester Street onto Palace Street, they looked down a long expanse of open ground that terminated at the Governor's Palace. One contemporary described the vista: "Toward the center of the city . . . is the Governor's Palace, very well built, very spacious, with a big lawn . . . which forms a pretty avenue." Rows of catalpa trees planted one hundred feet apart flanked the green.

The spacious homes built here after mid-century on large lots gave this part of Williamsburg a more residential air than the densely developed section of town near the Capitol. These well-built houses had a formal appearance that bespoke the education and civility that set their "gentle" owners apart from the "simple" artisan or tradesman. But such distinctions did not characterize Palace Street in the early years of the eighteenth century, when more modest one and one-half story houses shared the green with a tavern, a theater, and several tradesmen's shops.

Even after mid-century, when wealthy Virginians began to reshape the style of their houses in keeping with newly acquired refined manners, Palace Street did not become completely residential. From the 1730s on, unsightly piles of coal used to fuel the Geddy forge and foundry were in full view in the backyard of the James Geddy House on the corner of Palace and Duke of Gloucester Streets. In the 1760s, a lead manufactory was in operation beyond the Wythe property; by the 1770s, a busy coachworks was located behind the Elkanah Deane House. In the eighteenth century, polite society had not yet chosen to remove itself completely from the presence of the workaday world, and mixed residential neighborhoods like that around Palace Street were common.

Behind the houses on Palace Street, as elsewhere in Williamsburg, lived and worked the town's slaves. Signs of their presence—the currycombs of the grooms, the pots and pans of the cooks, and the pails of the housemaids—could be found all around these work areas. By the time of the Revolution, fully half of the town's population was black.

Here and there, tucked into corners or hidden in lofts above kitchens, stables, and other outbuildings, were the slaves' scant personal possessions: a straw-filled mattress, one or two extra pieces of clothing, an occasional fiddle or banjo. These few material goods only begin to suggest the full cultural life that Africans and their descendants created in the New World. In Williamsburg's backyards, black men and women courted, married, and reared children. They told African folk tales adapted to life in Virginia, taught their children how to cope with the harsh realities of slavery, and attempted to subvert the system by harboring runaway slaves.

William Levingston bought three lots at the corner of Palace and Nicholson Streets in 1716. Soon afterward, he built a house,

■ *Thomas Everard House*   Thomas Everard Office

kitchen, and other outbuildings. He also constructed a playhouse and laid out a bowling green. Today, the reconstructed **Levingston Kitchen** is all that remains on the site.

Levingston briefly operated a tavern at his house next door. He soon encountered financial difficulties and had to mortgage the property. The building continued to be used periodically. In 1736, "the young Gentlemen of the college" performed *The Tragedy of Cato*. Other plays were also presented.

This location changed in appearance and character through the years. By the mid-1730s, Dr. George Gilmer, a successful apothecary-surgeon, had acquired the property, moved into the house, and built an apothecary shop on the corner.

The open-air ■**Play Booth Theater** is located on the site of the first theater, which was active in the 1720s and 1730s. Archaeologists have unearthed the foundations of Levingston's playhouse. It measured eighty-six and one-half feet long by thirty feet wide and stood at least two stories high, about the same size as English provincial theaters of the period. In 1718, to celebrate the birthday of King George I, Governor Spotswood sponsored the first play known to have been staged at the theater.

In 1745, Dr. Gilmer sold the theater to a group of subscribers who gave it to the city to be remodeled for a courthouse. The "Hustings Court" (Williamsburg's municipal court) met here until the city and James City County joined in erecting the brick Courthouse on Market Square in 1770. About the same time,

the old playhouse was demolished.

The Play Booth Theater is similar to theaters erected for fairs and race days in England. Although performances sometimes attracted a boisterous, rowdy audience, the gentry also frequented playhouses—both Thomas Jefferson and George Washington attended plays in Williamsburg. In the eighteenth century, the theater was an important civilizing influence that educated people in socially acceptable ways to behave and edified them with dramas of virtue tried and virtue triumphant.

Today, actors at the Play Booth Theater present scenes from plays popular in Williamsburg before the American Revolution.

In 1788, St. George Tucker bought the house that Levingston had built. Tucker moved it to a more desirable location fronting on Market Square, which had, since the 1750s, become an increasingly important focus of town life.

John Brush, gunsmith, armorer, and first keeper of the Magazine on Market Square, built the ■**Thomas Everard House** on this property in 1718. After Brush died in 1726, it had several different owners.

Dancing master and painter William Dering bought the house in 1742. Although he was not a member of the gentry himself, Dering associated with the upper classes. By the mid-eighteenth century, planters were turning to dancing masters because they wanted to learn the elaborate manners that an increasingly fashion-conscious society valued. The ability to dance a minuet in the Governor's Palace or the Apollo Room at

Levingston Kitchen

the Raleigh Tavern meant that a person was a cultured member of polite society.

Thomas Everard arrived in Virginia as an orphan apprentice in the 1730s. Later a respected and wealthy local leader, Everard acquired the property about 1755 and lived there for twenty-five years. He was the clerk of the York County Court for nearly forty years, twice served as mayor of Williamsburg—in 1766 and 1771—and was on the vestry of Bruton Parish Church. Everard served as deputy clerk of the General Court from the 1740s until the Revolution.

The Thomas Everard House as originally constructed was a timber-framed one and one-half story building typical of the houses built here in the early years of the eigh-

teenth century. It was covered with weatherboards that were prepared by hand-splitting four-foot lengths of oak boards. The roof was covered with clapboards instead of shingles. A section of the original roofing is still in place, protected over the centuries by the roof ridge of the north addition.

The house was later enlarged and embellished to reflect the standing of its owner and the changing taste by which a gentleman was judged. The addition of two wings at the back resulted in a U-shaped plan. Fine paneling and rich carving—probably executed by the joiner who worked at Carter's Grove plantation—are evidence of Everard's affluence and taste.

The yard between the house and the outbuildings is paved with the original bricks

discovered during the course of archaeological excavations. The wooden smokehouse and the brick kitchen are original buildings that have been restored. Everard's nineteen slaves lived and worked in these outbuildings. Today, an exhibit in the house focuses on Everard, his children, and his slaves.

■**THE GOVERNOR'S PALACE.** A description of the Governor's Palace begins on page 80.

The **Robert Carter House** on the west side of Palace Street was constructed by 1746.

MEET . . . BRISTOL

Callers at the front door of Thomas Everard's house were greeted by Bristol, Everard's black footman, who was dressed in livery. Bristol's uniform, a respectable suit trimmed with braid and brass buttons, was not as elegant as the livery worn by footmen at the Governor's Palace, however.

Everard had purchased Bristol, who was in his late twenties, from the estate of Governor Fauquier in 1768. The previous year Bristol had been baptized at Bruton Parish Church. The record of Bristol's baptism noted that he was a "new" slave, which indicates that he had recently arrived in Virginia, probably from the west coast of Africa. Everard owned other slaves—an elderly groom, two young men who waited on the table and did other chores, a cook, a laundress, and a housemaid.

As Everard's manservant, Bristol's main duty was to wait upon his master. In the morning, he shaved him and laid out his clothes. At mealtimes, he supervised the young men who brought food to the table and served it. When Everard went out during the day, Bristol usually accompanied him. In the evening, he turned down his master's bed, used a bed warmer to take the chill off the sheets, and saw that the fire was well banked for the night.

Bristol was intelligent. He knew how to read (although he could not write), so Everard relied on him to deliver messages, run errands, and purchase provisions for the household. Bristol was proud of his abilities and of the confidence his master placed in him, but he never forgot that he was a slave.

Bristol looked forward to running errands to the Palace. When he delivered his master's gift of fish and peaches to the governor, the butler tipped him generously. More important, Bristol's trips to the Palace often gave him the opportunity to visit with Venus, Everard's laundress, who had been hired out to Governor Botetourt, Hannah, who was part of the Palace staff during Fauquier's and Botetourt's tenure in office, and other slaves who worked there.

McKenzie's Store

It served as Governor Dinwiddie's residence while the Palace underwent repairs in 1751 and 1752.

The first known owner was Charles Carter, son of Robert "King" Carter, one of the wealthiest Virginians in the colony. Robert Carter Nicholas, another member of the prominent family, purchased it in 1753. Long a leader of the House of Burgesses and treasurer of the colony, Nicholas made the house his home until 1761, when he sold it to Councillor Robert Carter, his cousin.

Robert Carter and his family lived in the house for twelve years. Six of his seventeen children were born here. Finding the dwelling "not sufficiently roomy," the Carter family returned to their plantation, called Nomini Hall, in 1772.

The house and the brick outbuilding are original. Other dependencies—including the unusual "breezeway"—were reconstructed. The Robert Carter Kitchen is now one of several Colonial Williamsburg hotel facilities in the Historic Area.

At mid-century, Dr. Kenneth McKenzie owned and lived on this property with his family. He operated his shop, **McKenzie's Store,** on the site. Dr. McKenzie died in 1755. Among other bequests, he left to his "good friend Doctor James Carter having behaved in a very kind manner to me in my Sickness . . . my Skeleton." Items typical of those sold in the eighteenth century are available in McKenzie's Store.

The **Elkanah Deane House** was named for the Irish coachmaker who paid seven hundred pounds for the original dwelling, shop, and garden on this site in 1772. Deane may have been encouraged to move to Williamsburg from New York by Governor Dunmore. Deane advertised in the *Virginia Gazette* that he "had the Honour of making a Coach, Phaeton, and Chaise, for his Excellency the Right Honourable the Earle of Dunmore."

The same issue of the newspaper carried an advertisement from Joseph Beck, a staymaker in New York City. Beck encouraged the "Ladies of Virginia" to give their orders for stays to Mrs. Deane, who would "take their Measures" and forward them to New York. Beck promised satisfaction.

Tree box topiary and small-leaved lindens are features of the Elkanah Deane House garden, which is open to ticket holders.

Behind the Elkanah Deane House on Prince George Street is the ■**Elkanah Deane Shop.** In the eighteenth century, the shop was the scene of carriage making on a considerable scale. Wheelwrights, blacksmiths, and harnessmakers were among the artisans who worked together to make carts, wagons, riding chairs, and carriages. Today, the shop is open seasonally.

George Wythe, one of the most influential Americans of his era, lived in the brick ■**George Wythe House** on the west side of Palace Street. His father-in-law, Colonel Richard Taliaferro, is believed to have designed the house. In his will, Taliaferro gave George

*Robert Carter House

Robert Carter Office

■ *George Wythe House*

and Elizabeth Wythe use of the property for life. Wythe lived in the house from about 1755, around the time he married Elizabeth Taliaferro, until 1791, when he moved to Richmond to serve as a judge on Virginia's Court of Chancery.

The Wythe House served as headquarters for Washington just before the siege of Yorktown. Rochambeau occupied it for several months while French troops were stationed in Williamsburg after Cornwallis's surrender in 1781.

Perhaps one of the grandest and most impressive private dwellings in town, the Wythe House represented the aspirations of the Virginia gentry during the second half of the eighteenth century. The plan of the house consists of four rooms on each of two full stories, with both floors centrally divided by a large stair passage. Two great chimneys rise between the paired rooms, thus affording a fireplace in all eight. The smaller windows in the second story have the same number of panes, or "lights," as those on the first floor, a device that increases the apparent size of the house. The exterior exhibits some of the best masonry

work in town, featuring Flemish bond brickwork enframed with rubbed jambs, corners, and water table, and gauged-brick belt course and splayed brick arches.

Although little is known about the specific personal property of George and Elizabeth Wythe, the house has been furnished with objects typically found in comparable Virginia gentry homes. Architectural and documentary evidence suggests that this dwelling was once wallpapered virtually throughout. The yellow ocher trim color, discovered through recent paint analysis, complements the brightly colored wallpaper exhibited in the house. A comprehensive study of wallpaper usage in colonial Virginia provided the documentation for the wide variety of patterns and colors used throughout the building.

Behind the house, a symmetrical garden plan divides the property into distinct areas. Archaeological excavations established the locations of major outbuildings in the service yard, which is adjacent to the side street. Among the reconstructed frame outbuildings are a smoke house, kitchen, laundry, lumber house, poultry house, well, dovecote, and stable. The pleasure garden is lined with tree box topiary and ends in an arbor of hornbeams. Two "necessary houses," or privies, are nearby. The orchard and the kitchen garden are on the south side of the property.

The house and gardens are open to ticket holders. Down hearth cooking is frequently demonstrated in the kitchen.

Elkanah Deane Shop

Elkanah Deane House

MEET . . . GEORGE WYTHE

Although the name of George Wythe (1726–1806) may be less familiar than those of other patriots, he was one of the most influential men of the Revolutionary era. As a member and then clerk of the House of Burgesses, Wythe (rhymes with "Smith") helped lead the patriot movement in Virginia. As one of the colony's delegates to the Continental Congress, he supported independence at Philadelphia. His name appears first among Virginia signers of the Declaration of Independence. Two years later, he helped revise Virginia's laws.

George Wythe's influence as a teacher of law and adviser equaled his distinguished record of public service. He probably did more to shape Thomas Jefferson's ideas than any other man. Jefferson studied law under Wythe and later referred to him as "my faithful and beloved Mentor in youth, and my most affectionate friend through life." Wythe bequeathed his "books and small philosophical apparatus" and his "silver cups and goldheaded cane" to Jefferson.

In 1779, Wythe was appointed to the newly established chair of law at the College of William and Mary, becoming the first individual to hold such a chair in an American university. His students included John Marshall, who made an indelible mark on the interpretation of the U. S. Constitution as chief justice of the Supreme Court from 1801 to 1835.

Wythe probably moved into the George Wythe House after he married Elizabeth Taliaferro (pronounced "Tolliver") around 1755. His father-in-law, Colonel Richard Taliaferro, who is believed to have designed the dwelling, bequeathed the couple use of the property for life. Elizabeth Wythe died in 1787, but Wythe continued to live in the house until 1791, when he resigned his professorship and moved to Richmond to serve as a chancery judge.

George Wythe opposed slavery in principle and freed some of his slaves during his lifetime. He taught at least two of his slaves to read.

Wythe died in 1806. He likely was poisoned by George Wythe Sweeney, a ne'er-do-well grand-nephew who lived with him. Sweeney probably expected a substantial inheritance, but Wythe lived long enough to disinherit him. Sweeney was never convicted, in part because it was illegal in Virginia for Lydia Broadnax, Wythe's free black housekeeper and an eyewitness to the crime, to testify against a white man.

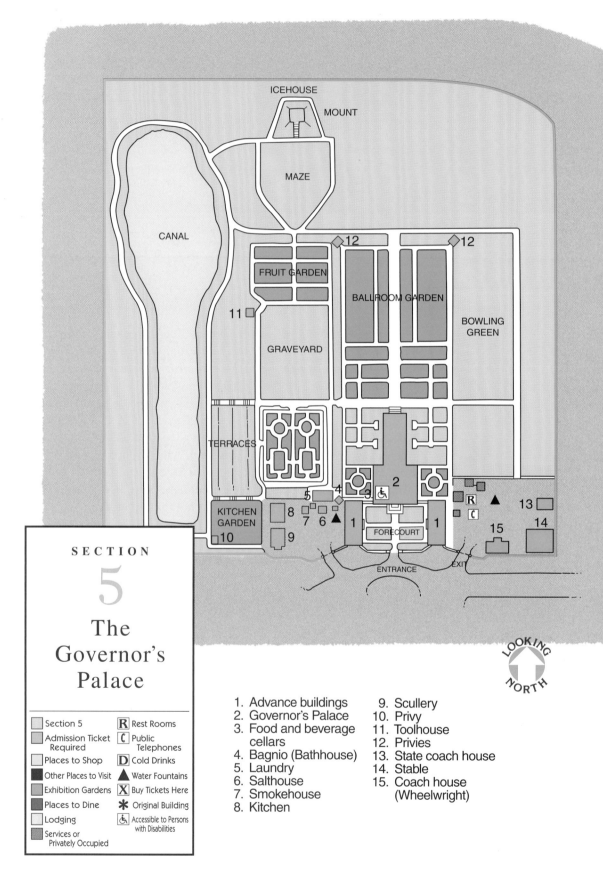

ICEHOUSE

MOUNT

MAZE

CANAL

FRUIT GARDEN

11

GRAVEYARD

12

12

BALLROOM GARDEN

BOWLING GREEN

TERRACES

KITCHEN GARDEN

10

4

5

8

7 6

1

2

3

FORECOURT

1

R

C

13

15

14

ENTRANCE

EXIT

LOOKING NORTH

SECTION

5

The Governor's Palace

☐ Section 5	**R** Rest Rooms	
☐ Admission Ticket Required	**C** Public Telephones	
☐ Places to Shop	**D** Cold Drinks	
■ Other Places to Visit	▲ Water Fountains	
☐ Exhibition Gardens	**X** Buy Tickets Here	
☐ Places to Dine	✱ Original Building	
☐ Lodging	♿ Accessible to Persons with Disabilities	
☐ Services or Privately Occupied		

1. Advance buildings
2. Governor's Palace
3. Food and beverage cellars
4. Bagnio (Bathhouse)
5. Laundry
6. Salthouse
7. Smokehouse
8. Kitchen
9. Scullery
10. Privy
11. Toolhouse
12. Privies
13. State coach house
14. Stable
15. Coach house (Wheelwright)

∎THE GOVERNOR'S PALACE

At the time of its completion in 1722, the residence of Virginia's royal governor was considered one of the finest such buildings in British America. It is difficult to appreciate just how remarkable this building really was unless the rural character of the colony at the close of the seventeenth century is taken into consideration. In spite of previous attempts to legislate towns into existence, few real towns or centers of commerce existed in Virginia; instead, the colony was populated by widely scattered agricultural settlements that acquired goods through direct trade with shippers and necessary services as needed from rural tradespeople.

The majority of Virginians, even many who were relatively well-to-do, lived in one-story houses composed of no more than two or three rooms. The enclosing walls of these houses often consisted of posts set directly into the earth and given a crude covering of "riven," or split, boards. Interior plaster and glass windows were found only in houses of the "better sort." By today's standards, living conditions in Virginia at the close of the seventeenth century were modest indeed.

With its broad, straight thoroughfares and massive public buildings, Williamsburg represented a new beginning—a magnet around which the colony would gather itself and thrive. Unlike most towns in Europe, this new metropolis had been laid out around an orderly ensemble of public buildings related to one another in a grand overall scheme.

The Palace was an important element in this great civic design. Sited at the end of a broad, imposing green, the governor's residence terminated the primary north-south axis of the town. The high visibility and symmetrical formality of this complex did much to re-

inforce the importance of the governorship in the eyes of Virginians.

Alexander Spotswood assumed the lieutenant governorship with apparent relish in 1710. More than any other of his contemporaries, Spotswood was determined that the new metropolis (and the governor's house in particular) should affirm the dignity and authority of the colony's educational, religious, and governmental institutions.

Soon after he arrived in Williamsburg, Spotswood set about to effect a series of improvements at the Palace, all of which were intended to amplify its grandeur and enhance his own posture as the Crown's appointed representative. The formal vista along Palace Street toward Francis Street, the elaborate gardens with a canal and falling terraces, the enclosed forecourt with its iron gate and royal heraldic beasts, the magnificent display of arms in the entrance hall, and the elegant appointments of the upper middle room, where the governor received petitioners, were features that appear to have been introduced during Spotswood's time.

From the foot of the green at Duke of Gloucester Street to the inner sanctum of Spotswood's elaborate upper middle room, the

Palace complex was a carefully orchestrated procession of spaces moving toward and culminating in the presence of the man sworn to uphold the authority of the English monarch in Virginia. The architectural setting of the governor's residence was intended to instill in the colonists respect for executive power and prerogative.

The construction of the Governor's Palace began in 1706, during the administration of Governor Edward Nott. In June of that year, following repeated exhortations from the Crown, the General Assembly voted to build a residence for the governor and appropriated three thousand pounds toward its erection.

Construction proceeded slowly, however, and the house was little more than an enclosed shell when Spotswood arrived in June 1710. Almost immediately the new governor took charge of the project, pushing it forward vigorously. It was almost certainly at his urging that the Assembly enacted additional legislation providing for the enclosure of the forecourt and gardens and considered further recommendations for "rendering the new House Convenient as well as Ornamental." In October 1711, William Byrd of Westover plantation strolled across town to view the new house, where he saw a magnificent display of weapons in the entrance hall, "nicely posited," as one observer put it, "by the ingenious contrivance of Colonel Spotswood."

Spotswood had moved into the house by 1716, although the work continued for another six years. In the meantime, the governor turned his attention to the gardens, where, in the western part, he laid out a series of terraces that descend to a canal below. Before long, however, members of the Assembly expressed alarm at the money being spent for these refinements. In disgust, Spotswood removed himself entirely from any further in-

volvement with the house and grounds.

The house was finally completed by 1722, but it is clear from the journals of the Assembly that minor repairs and even alterations continued to be made on a regular basis. The Palace had fallen into such "ruinous condition" by 1751 that Lieutenant Governor Robert Dinwiddie was forced to take up quarters next door at the house owned by Dr. Kenneth McKenzie (now the Robert Carter House) while extensive repairs were undertaken. By 1752, the Palace had been sufficiently rehabilitated to receive the governor and his household. The real construction work had only

The entrance hall to the Governor's Palace

begun, however. During the ensuing months, a rear wing encompassing the present ballroom and supper room was erected under the supervision of Richard Taliaferro, who was also responsible for the construction of the George Wythe House.

The creation of two large rooms for public entertainments coincided with the construction of similar spaces elsewhere in Williamsburg. The "great room" at Wetherburn's Tavern, where Governor Dinwiddie was first entertained after taking office, is believed to have been completed in 1751, as was the Apollo Room at the Raleigh Tavern. Such rooms were being added to private residences as well. The elaborate downstairs room at the Peyton Randolph House appears to date from the same era.

This new desire for large rooms suited to public entertainments echoed a similar trend

𝔅ecoming 𝒜mericans
Our Struggle to Be Both Free and Equal

THE FIRST CONSUMER REVOLUTION

Some programs in the Historic Area examine the changes that simultaneously revolutionized trade and technology and ultimately transformed peoples' standards and styles of living at all levels of society.

During the Middle Ages everyday domestic life among all classes except the nobility involved little in the way of clothing, furniture, and other household equipment. A person's reputation was measured by the land, labor, and livestock everyone knew he owned. By 1700, however, growing numbers of ordinary people in northern Europe and America began demanding and acquiring newly available consumer goods, using services, and engaging in social, recreational, and educational activities that went far beyond meeting or improving their basic physical needs.

Seeking respectability within an increasingly mobile society, successful image makers in Virginia dressed in the latest London fashions and built houses suitable for entertaining. They furnished those houses with new, specialized forms of furniture. They took tea from fashionable tea wares. Adults and children learned the rules of behavior that reaffirmed their social positions and differentiated them from their "inferiors." By mid-century local tradesmen and merchants—supported by advances in British business practices and industrial technology—offered an ever-increasing variety of consumer goods and services.

Widespread possession of store-bought culture, combined with etiquette book manners, contributed to a novel idea: equality, the belief in everyone's equal worth and right to pursue a better life. Yet some rejected the new materialism and the notion of equality. Others—especially the poor and slaves and servants—were disadvantaged by it. Resulting clashes between the haves and have-nots, slaves and free, men and women, country and city, and different religious groups were resolved in many ways. The widely shared experience of consumption eventually helped Americans of varying backgrounds express with a single voice their opposition to Parliament and its unjust laws.

in England. In 1756, English architect Isaac Ware noted that the addition of a "great room" to private residences had become commonplace, complaining that such an addition "always hangs from one end, or sticks to one side, of the house, and shews to the most careless eye, that, though fastened to the walls it does not belong to the building."

After the completion of the ballroom wing, few changes of any importance occurred in or around the Palace until the arrival of Norborne Berkeley, Baron de Botetourt, in 1768. Shortly after assuming his post, the governor launched a thorough program of redecoration that is reflected in the furnishings and exterior appointments of the Palace as visitors see it today.

With the coming of the American Revolution, Virginia's last royal governor, John Murray, fourth Earl of Dunmore, fled Williamsburg. The Palace then served as a residence for the first two governors of the new Commonwealth of Virginia, Patrick Henry and Thomas Jefferson. It was probably during his residence in Williamsburg that Jefferson prepared a series of drawings to guide in remodeling the Palace. His proposed changes were never carried out, however, because the seat of government—and the governor's residence—moved to Richmond in 1780.

American forces used the vacant Palace as a hospital following the siege of Yorktown. The orchard terrace overlooking the canal became a burial ground for 156 American soldiers. On the night of December 22, 1781, fire broke out in the Palace, and in three hours it had burned to the ground. Shortly afterward, all that remained of the central structure's charred hulk was pulled down and the bricks were sold. Within a few short months, the once-great Palace of Virginia's royal governors had become only a memory, its flanking advance buildings and outlying dependencies tangible reminders of its vanished magnificence.

In the eighteenth century, a liveried footman showed callers at the Palace into the entrance hall, where the royal coat of arms and ornamental arrangements of weapons represented the authority by which the governor ruled. In England, similar arrangements could be seen in the country houses of important men, at the Tower of London, and especially in the guard chambers of royal residences such as Hampton Court and Windsor Castle.

Like those royal guard chambers, the hall at the Palace functioned as a screening area where visitors wishing to see the governor were "sorted out." In the case of Lord Botetourt's household, William Marshman, the butler, supervised this process. Marshman had his office in the pantry to the left of the front door. From this vantage point, the butler managed the household staff that consisted of twenty-five servants and slaves. Hanging on the door is a ring of keys, a reminder that Marshman also controlled access to the governor's valuable collection of silver and to his stocks of wine and food in the cellar. Beside the library table where household accounts were kept is a bed in which the butler would have slept in order to secure the contents of this important room.

Many if not most visitors would have been shown into the parlor on the right, where they waited their turn to see the governor. The serviceable leather upholstery on the chairs in the parlor reflects the role of this space as a waiting room of sorts. Visitors would have found the numerous scripture prints on the walls both entertaining and edifying.

Prominent persons having particularly important business probably proceeded upstairs immediately for an audience with His Excellency. Moving through the entry hall and up the wide staircase, they approached the governor's elegant upper middle room, no doubt impressed by the grand procession of spaces with their ornamental displays of firearms and swords. At the head of the stair a visitor might pause expectantly in another waiting area until the time came for him to be received by the governor.

Beyond a final set of doors, the governor himself received visitors and transacted business amid considerable pomp in the elaborately appointed middle room. Strange as it may sound today, this ceremony, called a "levee," was a customary practice in Europe among men of power and influence. No doubt the formality of these occasions effectively portrayed the governor of colonial Virginia as a dignified and potent leader.

Those who enjoyed a close friendship with the governor might be invited into his bedchamber on the right, or, in the case of his most intimate associates, into the library beyond it. Because Lord Botetourt was a bachelor, he is likely to have designated the two bedchambers on the east for the use of visiting dignitaries such as Governor and Mrs. William Tryon of North Carolina, guests at the Palace in June 1769.

Not everyone calling at the Palace sought a private audience with the governor. Many attended him in his dining room, an area dedicated as much to business and politics as to meals. Lord Botetourt's dining room contained such clerical necessities as a small reading desk, a library table, and a mahogany desk that held public and private papers.

The governor's dining room was a male enclave from which ladies typically withdrew after meals, leaving the men to their bottles. In some cases, the decor of dining rooms in colonial Virginia reflected their masculine character. At Mt. Airy, Colonel John Tayloe covered the dining room walls with portraits of English racehorses.

Food brought over from the kitchen on covered pewter platters was transferred to china and silver serving pieces and garnished in the little middle room before being taken into the dining room across the passage.

Many visitors at the Palace enjoyed the

A glass pyramid dressed for the dessert course graces the table in the Palace dining room.

governor's entertainments. From the entrance hall guests passed through the set of double doors leading into the ballroom, where dances, or "routs" (as those occasions were sometimes called), took place.

Among the most fashionable and up-to-date rooms in the building, the ballroom and supper room became a stage on which the governor and his guests acted out the latest forms of etiquette and displayed themselves as being in touch with the world's most fashionable and civilized conversation and manners. Early in the eighteenth century, such an event would have involved a relatively small group of people, all engaged in a single activity in one room. Later in the century, however, assemblies included many more guests and featured a variety of activities going on in separate rooms. While people danced in one room, refreshments or a light supper might be served in another.

At the far end of the supper room a last pair of doors leads visitors into a formal garden resembling those found on many English estates during the early eighteenth century. Quite often those formal gardens served to frame pleasing views of distant pastoral scenery. This distant landscape, called a "park," was in many cases planted with clumps of trees arranged informally for a picturesque effect. Grazing cattle or a herd of deer usually completed the scene. By providing pleasant prospects, or vistas, to be enjoyed from near the house, the park functioned as an important adjunct to the formal garden.

Just such a park, which encompassed sixty-three acres, complemented the governor's gardens. Like many of its English counterparts, this park was visible from a mount in the formal garden or as visitors looked northward through the delicate tracery of the great wrought-iron gate. Governor Botetourt made occasional excursions into the park, enjoying its idyllic beauty from a special horse-drawn vehicle called a park-chair. Governor Dunmore seems to have favored the park for morning walks.

The formal garden with its manicured plantings was equally important as a source of pleasurable recreation. Here gentlemen might stroll along fragrant walks, trading pleasant flatteries with the ladies or perhaps continuing a conversation begun over dinner. Above all, however, these impressive gardens helped to present the governor as a refined and important man. In this respect, they functioned as an extension of the house and mirrored its formal character.

Farther from the house, in the western-most part of the garden, Spotswood's terraces, planted in a less formal manner than the rest of the garden, fall gently to the fish pond below. Spotswood capitalized on the topographic variety of the site, an approach to gardening that gained favor in England as designers began to move away from the rigid formality of an earlier age.

The stables and carriage house in the east yard served the transportation needs of the household. Lord Botetourt's state coach, a heavily gilded ceremonial vehicle in which the governor rode to the Capitol to open sessions of the General Assembly, was kept in the coach house. The elegance of His Excellency's coach prompted one visitor to comment on the tendency of Virginians "to adopt ideas of royalty and magnificence."

These service yards were also the centers of social life for the governor's household staff. As such, although they were less elegant than the ballroom, they were no less important.

The service yards are located to the east and west of the advance buildings that flank the Palace. The elegance of the governor's residence did not just happen; it was the product of hard work by many servants—butlers, footmen, maids, cooks, laundresses, gardeners, grooms, and laborers. The kitchen, scullery, laundry, and other support buildings involved in the task of maintaining the household are in the west yard. Of special interest is the hexagonal "bagnio," or bathhouse, a luxury rarely found elsewhere in Virginia. The butler had direct access to this entire service area by way of the mansion's west door.

Today, the ■Wheelwright demonstrates his trade in the stable area. In the eighteenth century, wheeled vehicles of every kind—wheelbarrows, riding chairs, carriages, and carts—were needed to move people or possessions from place to place. Wheeled vehicles of every description could be seen in the streets of Virginia's colonial capital.

The wheelwright must craft precise woodworking joints to bring the hub, spokes, and rim sections together into a perfectly round wheel. These parts are compressed tightly by an iron tire around the wheel's circumference to give it strength and durability. In the shop today, the wheelwrights produce wheels for the vehicles used in the Historic Area.

The ■Kitchen is the site of frequent demonstrations of the high cooking arts of a British kitchen in America.

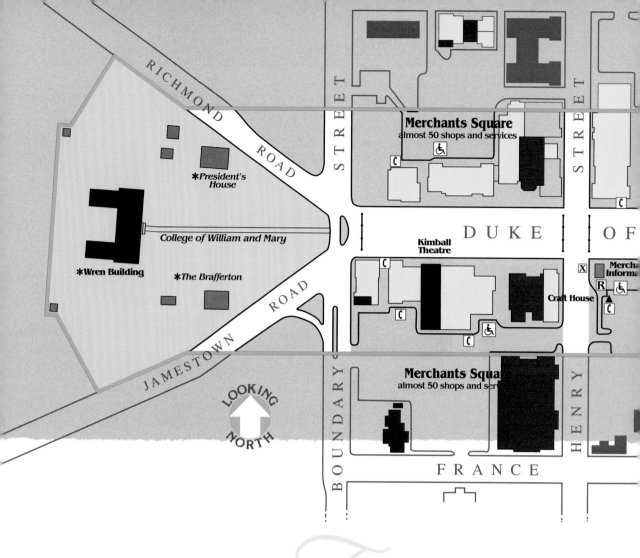

FROM PALACE STREET TO THE COLLEGE OF WILLIAM AND MARY

An asterisk (*) indicates that a building is an original eighteenth- or nineteenth-century structure. A ■ indicates that you need an admission ticket to see an attraction.

For most of the seventeenth century, what is now Williamsburg was little more than a winding horsepath faced by a tavern, a few stores, and several houses. Two important institutions fostered the growth of this part of the street. The first, Bruton Parish Church, was located here in 1674. The second, the colony's new college named to honor King William and Queen Mary of England,

was chartered in 1693. These two institutions, less than a half-mile apart, drew workers, artisans, and businessmen to Middle Plantation, the sparsely settled outpost that had been established in 1633 on the ridge between the James and York Rivers.

The appeal of locating the center of government near the colony's center of learning was partly responsible for the General

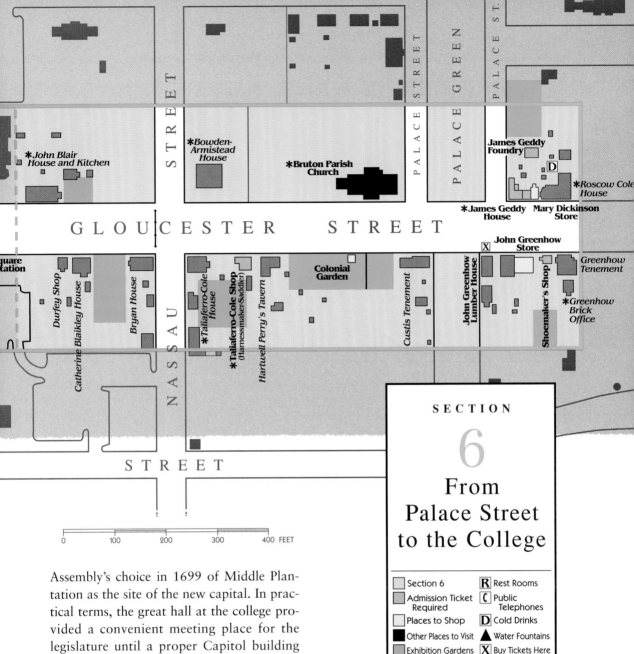

*John Blair House and Kitchen

*Bowden-Armistead House

S T R E E T

*Bruton Parish Church

P A L A C E   S T R E E T

S T R E E T

P A L A C E   G R E E N

P A L A C E   S T.

James Geddy Foundry

D

*Roscow Cole House

*James Geddy House

Mary Dickinson Store

John Greenhow Store

X

G L O U C E S T E R   S T R E E T

quare tation

Durfey Shop

Catherine Blaikley House

Bryan House

N A S S A U

*Taliaferro-Cole House

*Taliaferro-Cole Shop (Harnessmaker-Saddler)

Hartwell Perry's Tavern

Colonial Garden

Custis Tenement

John Greenhow Lumber House

Shoemaker's Shop

Greenhow Tenement

*Greenhow Brick Office

S T R E E T

SECTION

6

From Palace Street to the College

☐ Section 6	**R**	Rest Rooms
☐ Admission Ticket Required	**C**	Public Telephones
☐ Places to Shop	**D**	Cold Drinks
■ Other Places to Visit	▲	Water Fountains
☐ Exhibition Gardens	**X**	Buy Tickets Here
☐ Places to Dine	✱	Original Building
☐ Lodging	♿	Accessible to Persons with Disabilities
☐ Services or Privately Occupied		

0   100   200   300   400 FEET

Assembly's choice in 1699 of Middle Plantation as the site of the new capital. In practical terms, the great hall at the college provided a convenient meeting place for the legislature until a proper Capitol building could be erected. A major transformation of the town, renamed Williamsburg in honor of the English monarch, began. The grounds of the Capitol were located about a mile east of the college, with Duke of Gloucester Street linking the two buildings. The old path was widened and straightened, and any buildings standing in the new roadway were removed.

This "uptown" section of Williamsburg took on a more residential appearance than the busier "downtown" blocks of Duke of Gloucester Street near the Capitol. After the government moved to Richmond in 1780, commercial activity at the eastern end of the street declined. The college and the Public Hospital became Williamsburg's major local institutions, and the focus of town life shifted to this part of the city.

James Geddy *Mary Dickinson*
House and Foundry *Store*

FROM PALACE STREET TO NASSAU STREET

From about 1737 to 1777, gunsmith James Geddy, Sr., and his sons lived at or operated shops on the site of the ▪**James Geddy House** and ▪**Geddy Foundry.** A good deal more than gunsmithing went on here, however. An inventory taken after Geddy's death lists shop equipment, including brasswork for guns, a turner's lathe, bullet molds, and gunsmith's, cutler's, and founder's tools. In 1751, Geddy's sons David and William advertised that they were carrying on these trades at the shop near the church.

In 1760, the widowed Anne Geddy sold the property to her son James, Jr., who set up shop as a silversmith, goldsmith, and watch repairer. He also sold and repaired jewelry and objects of silver. It was difficult to attract customers to a location so far away from the busy Capitol. In a 1771 advertisement, a concerned Geddy hoped that the reasonableness of his prices would "remove the Objection of his Shop's being too high up Town . . . and the Walk may be thought rather an Amusement than a Fatigue."

William Waddill, a journeyman silversmith and engraver, worked in Geddy's shop. In 1770, Waddill made eight silver handles, a large engraved nameplate, and sixteen escutcheons for Governor Botetourt's coffin. James Geddy, Jr., married Elizabeth Waddill, who probably was William's sister. A leader in the community, James Geddy was one of three artisans named to the Williamsburg common council.

The two-story L-shaped Geddy House dates from the 1760s. Its low-pitched roof without dormers and the front porch with balcony and doorway above are unusual features. Today, interpretations in the house focus on the domestic and commercial activities of the family of James Geddy, Jr.

The Geddys operated a foundry behind the house. In the eighteenth century, the yard around several busy forges would have been littered with piles of coal, mounds of slag, and assorted iron and brass waste. A foundry once again operates on the property as artisans cast objects in bronze, brass, pewter, and silver.

Mary Dickinson advertised millinery, jewelry, and other goods for sale "next Door to MR. JAMES GEDDY'S Shop, near the Church" in an October 1771 issue of the *Virginia Gazette*. Today, an elegant assortment of items is again available in the **Mary Dickinson Store.**

The frame **Greenhow Tenement,** across and down the street from the Geddy House, was once the property of John Greenhow, whose son sold it to printer and newspaper publisher Joseph Repiton in 1810.

In 1773, George Wilson & Company advertised the arrival of a "choice Cargo of the best sorts of English leather for all Manner of Mens Shoes and Pumps" at the ■ **Shoemaker's Shop.** Wilson must have had more business than he could handle, since he encouraged two or three journeymen shoemakers to apply to

him "next Door to Mr. Greenhow's Store in Williamsburg." By the end of the next year, however, the household furniture and working materials of George Wilson, deceased, were offered for sale.

An eighteenth-century shoemaker could turn out an average of one pair of shoes per day. He made them with round or pointed toes as fashion might decree, although he generally used a straight last—that is, without distinction between right and left. Today, tradespeople once again make shoes here using the tools and techniques of the eighteenth century.

One contemporary account described the home of John Greenhow, a merchant in Williamsburg from about 1755 to his death in 1787, as "a large and commodious Dwelling House." The adjoining **John Greenhow Store** is the most completely reconstructed eighteenth-century commercial space in Williamsburg. From the merchant's counting room in back to the freshly painted sign above the front door, the store is an authentic recreation of its eighteenth-century counterpart. Advertisements in the *Virginia Gazette* from 1766 to 1780 enabled researchers to identify the wide variety of goods that John Greenhow and his sons sold in their general store. Wrought iron, fabrics, cooper's items, tinware,

Greenhow Tenement   ■ *Shoemaker's Shop*

MEET . . . JOHN GREENHOW

According to his tombstone in Bruton churchyard, Greenhow was born November 12, 1724, and died August 29, 1787. Raised in Westmoreland County, England, he may be the same John Greenhow whose bankruptcy in nearby Lancaster, England, was announced in a 1752 issue of the *Universal Magazine.*

Greenhow's name first appeared in Virginia records about that time. By the 1760s, newspaper advertisements show that his house and store were located on Duke of Gloucester Street across from the Geddy property.

John Greenhow was an enterprising and far-ranging merchant. His eight-ton, three-man schooner, the *Robert,* regularly plied between the James River and Philadelphia, carrying peas, pork, lard, and butter northward. The return journey brought earthenware, flour, bread, bar iron, chocolate, coffee, iron skillets, saddletrees, soap, and furniture such as chairs, tables, and chests of drawers. Greenhow even operated a second store in Richmond.

Advertisements that listed the variety of imported goods stocked by John Greenhow appeared regularly in the *Virginia Gazette,* most especially before sessions of the General Court and the Court of Oyer and Terminer, which brought large numbers of people to town. Greenhow's stated policy of selling for "ready money only" was probably intended just for nonresidents. Had his account books survived, they undoubtedly would show that he occasionally sold goods to townspeople on credit.

"and almost every other useful article that can be thought of" are featured here again today.

Viewed from the street, the building appears to be in three segments. From left to right, there are a sloped-roof counting room and office for the proprietor, the entrance to the store, and the doorway to the **John Greenhow House.** The separate building to the right, whose gable end faces the street, is the **John Greenhow Lumber House.** It functioned as a stockroom for furniture, barrels, and odds and ends too bulky to keep in the

John Greenhow Store and House

John Greenhow Lumber House

Paths paved with shells crisscross the Custis Tenement garden in an intricate geometric pattern.

store itself. In eighteenth-century parlance, "lumber" meant "items in storage."

The generous size, layout, and exterior finish of the combination store and home and the lumber house are indicated on several early nineteenth-century fire insurance policies taken out by Greenhow's son Robert. The insurance plats also show that behind the Greenhow property the slope of the ravine—with its meadows, gardens, corn house, and other outbuildings—was put to an agricultural use typical of lots at this end of Duke of Gloucester Street.

The **Custis Tenement** stands on a lot that John Custis acquired in 1714. Custis also pur-

chased two lots to the immediate west, built structures on them, and rented the properties as tenements. Cabinetmaker Peter Scott's residence, for example, was located in the open lot west of the formal garden.

In 1746, Custis leased a house on this lot to carpenter John Wheatley for three years, during which time Wheatley was to maintain the dwelling in good repair and "continually to keep the Chimneys clean swept for fear of fire." He continued to rent the property through 1757, according to accounts presented in court by Martha Custis, the widow of Daniel Parke Custis, who had inherited the property from his father. The Widow Custis later married George Washington.

Just as English and European towns and villages had for centuries grown up around parish churches, so too did Middle Plantation. The tombs, gravestones, and site of a modest brick church completed in 1683 are reminders of the small seventeenth-century hamlet that was transformed into Williamsburg by Governor Nicholson's plan for a new city designed to be a fit seat for the colonial capital of Virginia.

Custis Tenement

In the late seventeenth century, before the college was built, **Bruton Parish Church** was the most important public building at Middle Plantation. Named for a town in Somerset, England, Bruton Parish was established here when several smaller parishes were joined together in 1674. Three years later, the vestry ordered that a church be built on the site. A small buttressed brick church was completed in 1683. Francis Louis Michel, a Swiss traveler who visited Williamsburg in 1702, left a sketch of the first Bruton Parish Church that shows that it had curvilinear end gables done in the Flemish manner. Its foundations are marked by granite posts northwest of the present church.

The small church was badly in need of repair by the early 1700s. Furthermore, it could not accommodate the many people who came to Williamsburg during "Publick Times," when the courts were convened. The vestrymen therefore petitioned the General Assembly "for their Generous contribution" toward building a new church. Lieutenant Governor Alexander Spotswood, an architectural enthusiast, pro-vided a "platt or draught of the Church," and the Assembly, which wanted a building more appropriate for the seat of government, appropriated two hundred pounds toward the cost. Begun in 1712, the cruciform Bruton Church has been in continuous use since 1715.

James Morris, carpenter, supervised the construction of Bruton Church. Other Williamsburg artisans also worked on the structure; for example, Lewis Delony built the original pews.

The chancel was extended twenty-two feet to the east in 1752, and an English organ was installed in 1755. The stone baptismal font reportedly was brought from an earlier church at Jamestown about this time. In 1769, local contractor Benjamin Powell was awarded the contract to build a new tower and steeple. The much darker shade of the bricks used in the tower contrasts with the soft salmon color of the brickwork of the main building. The bell, given to the parish by merchant James Tarpley in 1761, is still in use today.

From 1903 to 1907, under the direction of then-rector Dr. W. A. R. Goodwin, nineteenth-century changes were stripped from the church in order to return the interior to the way it had looked in the 1700s. A more complete restoration occurred in 1940. The building's

Bruton Parish Church

mined the annual taxes necessary to pay the minister's salary, provide relief for the poor of the parish, and repair the church. Free Virginians were required by law to attend divine services at least once each month and could be fined for failure to do so. All officeholders were obliged to conform to the established church, and all taxpayers—Anglicans and dissenters alike—were expected to support it and participate in its sacraments.

Divine services were held each Sunday morning. They included readings from the Book of Common Prayer, a sermon, and, four times a year, the taking of holy communion. Services were also held on Christmas Day, Good Friday, and various saint's days. It is thought that some favored house slaves sat with their owners in the pews.

Blacks in the parish also worshiped at Bruton Church. Tradition says that they sat apart in the north gallery, although it is possible they were relegated to floor space on the periphery or to back benches. By the end of the Revolution, more than one thousand slaves, many of them infants, had been baptized in Bruton Church.

Inspired by two black preachers, Gowan Pamphlet and Moses, a number of Williamsburg area blacks, most of them slaves, formed a church of their own after the Revolution. With a membership of five hundred, "the Baptist Church of black people at Williamsburg" was received into the Dover Baptist Association in 1793. A plaque marks the site of their church on Nassau Street opposite the Taliaferro-Cole stable.

The **Bowden-Armistead House,** completed in 1858 of Baltimore stock brick, is a good example of Greek Revival architecture. The iron fence that surrounds it was brought from Richmond.

Lemuel J. Bowden, a lawyer and president of the board of overseers of Eastern State Hospital, purchased the land on which the house stands from Bruton Parish. Many town

walls and window are original, as is the west gallery, where students from the college sat. The initials they carved in the handrail are still discernible.

The churchyard was surrounded by a brick wall in 1754. Many graves, including those of Governors Edward Nott and Francis Fauquier, are located in the churchyard, although in the eighteenth century it was more often the custom for people to be buried at home in private cemeteries. The Reverend Hugh Jones complained about this practice in 1724 because it meant he had to travel long distances to officiate at burials. Typical private plots can be seen today behind the Custis Tenement and the Taliaferro-Cole House across the street. Some of the table tombs in the churchyard were imported from England.

The state supported the Anglican church in colonial Virginia. Made up of twelve men, the vestry regulated church affairs and deter-

Bowden-Armistead House

residents considered Bowden, one of Williamsburg's few Northern sympathizers during the Civil War, to be a traitor and gave him the unflattering sobriquet of "Virginia Yankee." In 1874, the house was purchased from the Bowden estate by lawyer Robert T. Armistead. It is still owned by the Armistead family today.

At **The Colonial Garden and Nursery,** interpreters demonstrate eighteenth-century gardening techniques. Plant varieties found in Williamsburg during the colonial era and eighteenth-century-style tools and horticultural supplies are also for sale here.

Hartwell Perry's Tavern was named for Hartwell Perry, who owned and operated an "ordinary," as colonial taverns were sometimes called, on this site from the mid-1780s until he died about 1800. Previously, the land had been owned by John Custis, who built yet another tenement on the property and rented it in 1746 to joiner and cabinetmaker James Spiers.

The sign hanging out front is a "rebus." It depicts a deer, a well, and several pears.

"Hart" is another name for a deer, and an alcoholic beverage made from pears is called "perry"—so the sign stands for Hartwell Perry.

Despite a late nineteenth-century facade and earlier additions to the rear, the original ■**Taliaferro-Cole Shop** had remained essentially intact when the building was acquired for restoration.

Coachmaker Charles Taliaferro practiced his trade in Williamsburg for more than thirty years. He also operated a brewery and a warehouse, hired out boats, and sold foodstuffs and other supplies to outfit ships at nearby College Landing. He purchased this property in the early 1770s. The western section of the **Taliaferro-Cole House** dates from Taliaferro's period of ownership, but the restored house reflects the early 1800s, when Jesse Cole acquired the house and shop. Cole used the shop as a post office and general store. Today, the shop houses the trades of the harnessmaker and the saddler.

Hartwell Perry's Tavern   ■*Taliaferro-Cole Shop (Harnessmaker-Saddler)* *Taliaferro-Cole House*

John Blair House   *John Blair Kitchen*

FROM NASSAU STREET TO MERCHANTS SQUARE

A gable-roofed house probably built sometime after mid-century on the present site of the **Bryan House** survived until the twentieth century. At different times, it served as a grocery store, residence, and school.

William Blaikley and his wife, Catherine, lived in the **Catherine Blaikley House** next door. When he died in 1736, William bequeathed "unto my loving wife Catherine Blaikley, all my whole estate of lands, houses, negroes, goods, and chattels." Catherine, who apparently never remarried, remained at this address until her death in 1771 at the age of seventy-three. A remarkable woman, she was renowned as an "eminent Midwife . . . who, in the course of her Practice, brought upwards of three thousand Children into the world."

In April 1773, tailor Severinus Durfey announced his move to the house formerly occupied by Mrs. Blaikley. He used the **Durfey Shop** to the west for his tailoring activities and for other commercial purposes. The golden fleece of the signboard is the traditional symbol of a tailor's shop.

The **John Blair House and Kitchen** on the north side of Duke of Gloucester Street was the home of a prominent family of Virginians. The Reverend James Blair (1655–1743), founder and first president of the college of William and Mary, came to Virginia in 1685. His brother, Dr. Archibald Blair, arrived in 1690. Archibald's son, John Blair, Sr., received a legacy of ten thousand pounds from his uncle James, who left his library and five hundred pounds to the college.

John Blair, Sr. (1689–1771), a burgess and auditor general of the colony from 1728 to 1771, was appointed to the Council in 1745. Later, as president of the Council, he twice served as acting governor of the colony. His son, John Blair, Jr. (1732–1800), graduated from William and Mary and studied law at the Middle Temple in London. He was elected

Bryan House   *Catherine Blaikley House*   *Durfey Shop*

Becoming Americans
Our Struggle to Be Both Free and Equal

LAND

A key component of the eighteenth century was Virginians' quest for land ownership, Native Americans' desire to retain control of their ancestral homes, and the British government's developing imperial policies were resolved in the eighteenth century. Competition to possess the land shaped a number of fundamental American values.

Throughout the colonial period, the promise of land ownership lured a steady stream of European immigrants to the colony. By the mid-eighteenth century, Virginians had pushed westward, reaching the Ohio River Valley and Kentucky.

In their eagerness to claim the land, Virginians repeatedly came into contact—and conflict—with its native inhabitants. For native peoples, the land and its traditional uses were at the center of their culture. For colonists, land ownership was vital to their economic independence and social advancement.

As the capital of a vast territory, Williamsburg was the center of shifting networks of political, economic, diplomatic, and military relationships that linked colonial Virginia, Native American groups, other colonies, and France and Great Britain as each vied for control of the Ohio country and Kentucky.

In taking possession of the land for themselves, colonial Virginians altered the environment and initiated an exploitative ideology of land usage. The emergence of a large freeholding population fostered Americans' belief in individualism and the ideal of private land ownership. Even so, this privilege has yet to be extended to all Americans.

---

to the House of Burgesses and later became clerk of the Council. He sat on the committee that drew up Virginia's Declaration of Rights and first state constitution, and he served the new commonwealth as councillor, judge, and chief justice. In 1787, he represented Virginia at the Constitutional Convention, where he firmly advocated federal union, and in 1789, President George Washington appointed him to the United States Supreme Court.

The original, easterly part of the John Blair House was built early in the eighteenth century. It is one of the oldest houses in Williamsburg. Town tradition has it that the stone steps at both doors came from the Palace Street theater. The steps were added when the house was lengthened twenty-eight feet to the west sometime during the second quarter of the eighteenth century.

The kitchen, with its huge chimney, has been reconstructed. Between the kitchen and the street is a small formal herb garden that is open to ticket holders.

The 1782 Frenchman's Map shows quite a few buildings on the last block of Duke of Gloucester Street, an area that is now called **Merchants Square,** but little is known about the people who resided there or the structures in which they lived. Usually a tavern and other businesses catered to the needs of the faculty and students at the college.

Merchants Square Ticket Office, at the corner of South Henry and Duke of Gloucester Streets, is open daily for information and admission tickets.

Today Merchants Square is again a busy commercial and shopping district. The stores are modeled after eighteenth- and early nineteenth-century structures from Maryland and Delaware. More than sixty years old, Merchants Square is one of the first planned shopping centers in America.

The orderly and almost symmetrical area of the **College of William and Mary** yard at the western end of Duke of Gloucester Street forms an architectural unit in itself. The central structure is the **Wren Building,** with its massive chimneys and lofty cupola. Flanking it to the north and south are the **President's House** and **The Brafferton,** buildings apparently identical to one another in dimension and detail, although The Brafferton is actually somewhat smaller. The narrow, many-paned windows and steeply pitched roofs of these two buildings give a strong vertical accent to the architectural composition.

The College of William and Mary is the second oldest institution of higher education in the United States. It received a charter from King William and Queen Mary in 1693 after the General Assembly sent the Reverend James Blair to England to persuade the royal couple to found an Anglican college in the colony so that "the Church of Virginia may be furnish'd with a Seminary of Ministers of the Gospel." The college was also established in order "that the Youth may be piously educated in good Letters and Manners, and the Christian Faith may be propagated amongst the Western Indians."

In the eighteenth century, a higher education was not easily acquired in the colonies, so the few who attained it enjoyed considerable prestige. Plantation owners commonly entrusted their young sons to tutors who lived with the family. Occasionally, a few studied with a clergyman who augmented his income by running a small school. Young men then obtained a higher education by attending the College of William and Mary or going overseas to study at the universities of Oxford, Cambridge, or Edinburgh. Some read law at the Inns of Court in London.

Although the average enrollment during the

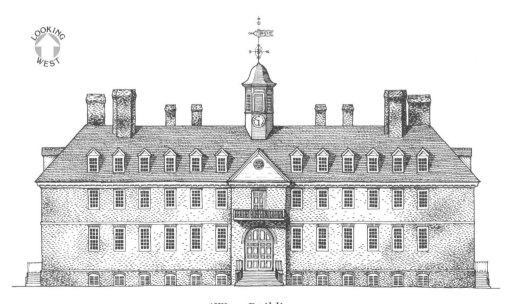

Wren Building

eighteenth century was less than one hundred, the College of William and Mary greatly influenced the intellectual life of Virginia. The college produced an extraordinary number of distinguished alumni, including Thomas Jefferson, John Marshall, and James Monroe.

Students at the college received a classical education. The grammar school admitted boys of about age twelve. They prepared for college-level work by mastering Latin and Greek as well as mathematics, geography, and penmanship. Latin was the language of both written and spoken classwork.

In addition to logic, rhetoric, and ethics, older students studied natural philosophy—mathematics, physics, and metaphysics. After four years of study in the school of philosophy, young men who submitted a written thesis and made a successful oral defense of it were awarded a Bachelor of Arts degree. Most students at the college in the eighteenth century left without taking a degree, however.

The faculty included such distinguished men as the Reverend Hugh Jones, mathematician, and Dr. William Small, professor of natural philosophy (science). "I know of no place in the world," wrote Jefferson in 1788, "while the present professors remain, where I would so soon place a son."

It was largely through the influence of alumnus Jefferson that the curriculum was broadened in 1779. To the old professorships of moral philosophy, natural philosophy, and mathematics were added new chairs of law

MEET . . . JOHN NETTLES

In the early 1770s, John Nettles, a young college student, was summoned before the faculty of the College of William and Mary for getting drunk at a Williamsburg tavern. He had committed a common offense, yet the master of the Indian school was clearly upset with Nettles. This promising young man had met the faculty's expectations. That he would risk all he had achieved by this misstep was alarming because Nettles was no ordinary student. He was a Catawba Indian, and he was expected to bring Christianity and civilization to his people.

Since the early eighteenth century, the college had enrolled Indian youngsters at The Brafferton, where they were taught reading, writing, and arithmetic. The young boys were also instructed in Christianity. And, most important, they were to experience firsthand the superiority of English culture. The faculty hoped that when the students returned home, they would continue to live like Englishmen and, by their example, lead their families to abandon their Indian ways.

The faculty's hopes were almost always disappointed. Once home, the young men reverted to their traditional ways. And so did John Nettles. In 1786, he was described as "a perfect Indian."

Although Nettles failed to keep to his instructors' expectations, he did fulfill the goals of the Catawbas. Within the year, the literate John Nettles was carrying messages to the colonial authorities, and he would act as an interpreter between his people and their white neighbors for the next forty years. By playing the middleman, the William and Mary-educated Nettles helped the Catawbas maintain their cultural autonomy in what for them was a hostile world.

The Wren Building is the oldest academic building in use in America.

and police, chemistry and medicine, ethics and belles lettres, and modern languages. The chair of divinity and the grammar school were discontinued. Although William and Mary had been founded as an Anglican college, the Reverend James Madison, its president at the time, explained, "It is now thought that Establishments in favor of any particular Sect are incompatible with the Freedom of a Republic."

The Wren Building bears the name of the distinguished English architect, Sir Christopher Wren, who may possibly have influenced its original design. Construction began in 1695. The building's front and its north wing, which contains a great hall, were completed by 1700. The chapel wing was added in 1732.

Although fires in 1705, 1859, and 1862 did serious damage, the massive exterior walls of the Wren Building are largely original. They have withstood not only flames but also the architectural modifications and structural alterations that were part of each rebuilding. The Wren Building now has the outward appearance that it showed from early in the eighteenth century until the fire of 1859. It was the first major Williamsburg structure to be restored by John D. Rockefeller, Jr.

The courtyard was originally intended to be enclosed within a quadrangular building, the two wings being joined across the far ends by a structure similar to the front side. Jefferson, an accomplished amateur architect, drew plans for an enlarged quadrangle, and

President's House

foundations had been laid when the outbreak of the Revolution put an end to the project. Some of those foundations still exist.

The president, the professors, and the master of the grammar school ate at the head table in the great hall, the dining room for the college. At the other tables, in descending order of status, sat the students, lesser faculty, "servitors and college officers," and, finally, the Indian master and his pupils. From the kitchen, directly below, the housekeeper saw to it that "plenty of Victuals" were "served up in the cleanest and neatest Manner possible" three times each day.

The House of Burgesses met in the great hall during the years 1700 to 1704 while the Capitol was under construction. The government of Governor Nicholson crowded all of its activities and offices into the building, "to the great disturbance of the college business," President Blair complained. The burgesses met there again from 1747 to 1754 while the Capitol was rebuilt after being gutted by fire.

Added in 1732, the chapel is evidence that the established Church of England played a central role in education as well as government in colonial Virginia. In the crypt below the chapel are buried Sir John Randolph; his sons, Peyton and John; Governor Botetourt;

Bishop James Madison; and several other distinguished Virginians.

Students began the day at 6 or 7 o'clock with morning prayer service in the chapel. Classes were held in the morning and again after midday dinner. Evening prayer, or evensong, was said at 5 P.M. A light supper followed, and the day ended when the whole student body gathered before the masters to be counted, blessed, and sent to bed.

The second-floor common room, where the professors and masters gathered to converse and relax, would today be called the faculty lounge or library. The president and masters met in the convocation room, familiarly known to generations of students as the "blue room," to conduct college business. They summoned students to the blue room to be commended or censured for their academic performance—or occasionally for their extra-curricular behavior.

Built in 1732–1733, the President's House has been the residence of every president of the College of William and Mary save one. Its first occupant, the Reverend James Blair, was the energetic Anglican clergyman who first induced the Virginia Assembly to favor the

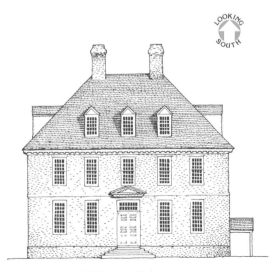

The Brafferton

This classroom was used by the master of the Grammar School to prepare boys twelve to sixteen for college.

erection of a college and then, in 1693, persuaded King William and Queen Mary to charter and endow it. He also supervised the construction of all the early buildings and selected the first faculty and curriculum. Blair served as president for half a century.

During the last stages of the Revolution, British General Cornwallis used the house briefly as his headquarters. French officers serving under General Rochambeau occupied the house for a short time after the Siege of Yorktown, causing accidental damage by fire. The French government allocated funds to repair the building.

When Robert Boyle, the noted British scientist, died in 1691, he left his personal property to charitable and pious uses at the discretion of his executors. They invested some of the funds in the manor of Brafferton in Yorkshire. President James Blair persuaded the executors to give most of the profits from

Brafferton to the College of William and Mary to be used for the education and conversion of Indian boys.

At first the Native American students had a classroom in the Wren Building and lodged elsewhere in the town. The Brafferton was completed for their use in 1723. Until the Revolution cut off revenue from the Boyle foundation, there were always some Indians—often a dozen or more—at the college. Most of them seem to have forgotten their prayers and their catechism after they left Williamsburg, however. So far as is known, not one of the Indians became a missionary as Boyle's executors had hoped.

The building suffered remarkably little damage over the years, although Federal troops ripped its interior woodwork from the walls and used it for firewood during the Civil War. The Brafferton today houses offices for the college.

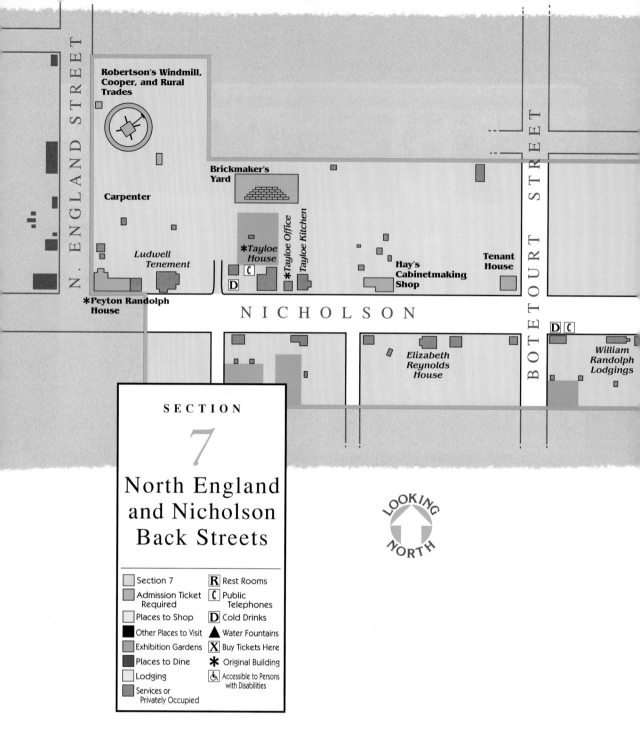

N. ENGLAND STREET

Robertson's Windmill, Cooper, and Rural Trades

Carpenter

Ludwell Tenement

***Peyton Randolph House**

Brickmaker's Yard

***Tayloe House**

Tayloe Office

Tayloe Kitchen

C

D

Hay's Cabinetmaking Shop

Tenant House

BOTETOURT STREET

N I C H O L S O N

Elizabeth Reynolds House

D C

William Randolph Lodgings

LOOKING NORTH

S E C T I O N

7

North England and Nicholson Back Streets

Section 7
R Rest Rooms
Admission Ticket Required
C Public Telephones
Places to Shop
D Cold Drinks
Other Places to Visit
▲ Water Fountains
Exhibition Gardens
X Buy Tickets Here
Places to Dine
* Original Building
Lodging
♿ Accessible to Persons with Disabilities
Services or Privately Occupied

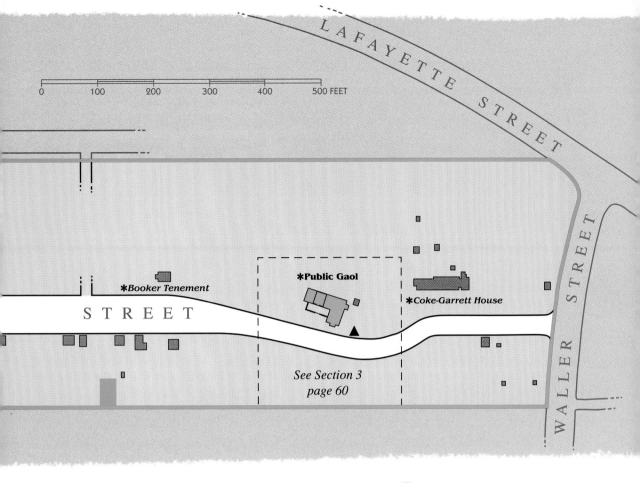

*See Section 3
page 60*

NORTH ENGLAND AND
NICHOLSON BACK STREETS

*An asterisk (*) indicates that a building is an original
eighteenth- or nineteenth-century structure. A ■ indicates
that you need an admission ticket to see an attraction.*

mixture of buildings—substantial town houses and modest dwellings, shops and stores, lodging houses and taverns—characterized North England, Nicholson, Waller, and Francis Streets in the eighteenth century. Structures on these back streets were generally spaced farther apart than those along Duke of Gloucester Street. Working sheds, smokehouses, dairies, kitchens (some with attics or lofts for slave quarters), poultry runs, livestock pens, stables, carriage houses, wood-piles, privies—all could be found in the back-yards of the colonial capital. This was the workaday world of Williamsburg, where slaves and white servants went about the drudgery of everyday life.

The dark red ■Peyton Randolph House at the corner of Nicholson and North England Streets was the home of one of the most prominent families in colonial Virginia.

The house has three parts. The oldest, which originally faced west onto North En-

■ *Peyton Randolph House*

gland Street, was built about 1718. Sir John Randolph and his family were living there in 1724 when he bought the lot and the one and one-half story house next door. In the mid-eighteenth century, the two were linked by a two-story central section that features a grand stairway and a monumental round-headed window. Inside the house is the best series of surviving paneled rooms in Williamsburg. Although most of the paneling is the usual yellow pine, the northeast room on the second floor of the oldest section is paneled completely in oak.

When he died in 1737, Sir John Randolph willed the house to his widow during her lifetime and then to his son Peyton. Sir John also left his library to Peyton, "hoping he will betake himself to the study of law." Thomas Jefferson bought the library after his cousin Peyton's death in 1775. Jefferson's library later became the nucleus of the Library of Congress. A number of Randolph's books have been identified by signature or by bookplate among the Jefferson collection there.

Peyton fulfilled his father's hopes and studied law at the Inns of Court in London. He was appointed attorney general of the colony of Virginia in 1744, elected to the House of Burgesses in 1748, became Speaker of the House in 1766, and presided over it at every

session in the crucial decade before the Revolution. In 1774, he traveled to Philadelphia, where he was elected unanimously to be president of the first Continental Congress.

In August 1774, just before the Continental Congress convened, legislators met at the Peyton Randolph House to determine what course Virginia's delegates should follow. Thomas Jefferson was ill and could not attend, but he sent his suggestions to his cousin Peyton, and they were read aloud to a group of patriots. Jefferson's document was soon printed and distributed as *A Summary View of the Rights of British America*. Too radical for some but moving to all, it was one of the influential tracts that led colonial Americans toward independence.

Mrs. Betty Harrison Randolph continued to live in the house after her husband's death. She relinquished it for a time during the Revo-

MEET . . . THE RANDOLPH FAMILY

The Randolphs were the first family of Williamsburg during the colonial period. Considered the most distinguished lawyer in the colony, Sir John Randolph (1693–1737) was the only colonial-born Virginian to be honored with knighthood for his services to the Crown.

Sir John's sons Peyton (ca. 1721–1775) and John (1727–1784) attended the College of William and Mary, trained at the Inns of Court, and then practiced law. Peyton became attorney general within a year of his return to Virginia after completing his legal training in England. John succeeded his brother in that post when Peyton was elected Speaker of the House of Burgesses.

The Randolphs lived comfortably and married well. After their wedding in 1745, Peyton and his bride, Elizabeth Harrison of Berkeley plantation, resided in the house he had inherited from his father. John and Ariana Randolph lived in a handsome dwelling located at the southern end of South England Street. John and Ariana entertained in style, and their house became a popular literary and social center frequented by the town's and the Virginia colony's elite, including the governors and their families.

Although both Peyton and John were political moderates who hoped for reconciliation with the mother country, they took opposing sides in the years before the American Revolution. From the mid-1760s, John sided with the Crown. He became a close friend of Governors Fauquier and Botetourt and was a confidant of Governor Dunmore. Peyton supported the colonists' cause, presiding over sessions of the first and second Continental Congresses.

The war divided the Randolphs in another way. John and his wife and daughters sailed "home" to England in September 1775, but his son, Edmund, remained in America, serving as an aide-de-camp to General Washington.

Peyton Randolph died unexpectedly in Philadelphia of an apoplectic stroke in 1775. Embittered, John lived in England until his death in 1784, periodically petitioning Parliament to recoup the losses he incurred when he left Virginia.

History has judged the Randolph brothers—the elder as a patriot leader, the younger as "John the tory."

lution so that the Comte de Rochambeau could establish his headquarters in the building before the Yorktown campaign. General Lafayette visited the house when he came to Williamsburg in 1824.

Today, the Peyton Randolph House is furnished with English and American antiques, including several pieces of Randolph family silver. Visitors learn about the choices members of the household—Peyton Randolph, Betty Randolph, and their slaves—made as the colonies moved toward revolution. Sites and activities behind the house feature both urban and rural activities.

In the eighteenth century, someone peering over the fence behind the Peyton Randolph House would have seen slaves bustling about, cooking and preparing food or stitching, laundering, and drying clothes and household linens. Betty Randolph, the mistress of the house, supervised them. Other slaves tended the garden or worked in the stable located toward the rear of the property.

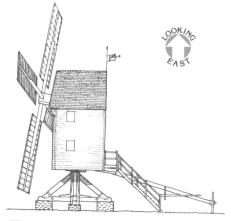

■ *Robertson's Windmill*

Randolph's inventory, taken in 1776, suggests that his slaves spun thread and yarn and made candles because it lists a parcel of tallow and twenty-three candle molds, five flax wheels, four reels, two spinning wheels, and parcels of wool, hemp, and flax. The inventory also includes twenty-seven slaves, some of whom may have been hired out to work elsewhere in town, a fairly common practice in the eighteenth century.

Archaeologists have located a series of small structures north of the Peyton Randolph House near the street line that have been identified as outbuildings. When the property was offered for sale in 1783, an advertisement noted that it had "every necessary outhouse convenient for a large family, garden, and yard well paled in," and, along the north side of Scotland Street next to the Palace land, "stables to hold twelve horses and room for two carriages, with several acres of pasture ground."

Today, the ■Carpenter works behind the house, using eighteenth-century tools and methods to prepare materials and reconstruct the outbuildings. It took about as much time to erect a house in eighteenth-century Williamsburg as it does today, assuming you count only construction hours and not those required to prepare the building materials.

Much is shaped by hand. Joints are cut to connect the timbers, a stronger, more complicated process because the carpenter must chisel mortises and tenons instead of nailing the components. Large numbers of nails are used for weatherboards, floors, and roofs, however.

Behind the outbuildings is ■**Robertson's Windmill,** which has been reconstructed on a site owned early in the eighteenth century by William Robertson, clerk of the Council and one of early Williamsburg's leading citizens.

Colonial Virginians depended on local mills to grind the grain from which they made their bread, a staple of their diet that appeared at nearly every meal. Sometimes colonial householders bought cornmeal or flour for cash, or "ready money." If they brought their own grain to be ground, they might barter with the miller or agree to let him exact his time-honored one-sixth toll.

Robertson's Windmill is a post mill, so called because the whole superstructure revolves on top of a single huge post of hewed timber. The superstructure has two levels. The

MEET . . . EVE

Eve was a slave in the household of Peyton and Betty Randolph. She worked as Betty Randolph's personal maid. In 1776 Eve was appraised at one hundred pounds, making her one of the most valuable female slaves the Randolphs owned.

Each morning, Eve laid out her mistress's clothes and helped her dress. Throughout the day, she relayed Betty's instructions to the other slaves, fetched items for her, and ran errands in Williamsburg. At night she warmed her mistress's bedsheets with the warming pan and helped Betty prepare for bed.

Eve's days were long, for she rose before her mistress and retired after Betty did. During her limited free time, Eve often took her mending to the outbuildings behind the Randolphs' house. There she would spend time with her sons, Caesar and George, while she sewed. Eve treasured these moments with her children.

Although Eve played an important role in the day-to-day activities of the Randolph household, she could not keep her family intact. After Peyton Randolph died in 1775, Betty Randolph sold fifteen-year-old Caesar. Eve's only consolation was that Caesar's new owner lived in Williamsburg, enabling her to see her older son occasionally.

Eve resolved to do everything she could to protect ten-year-old George, who was still with her. When British soldiers occupied Williamsburg in June 1781, Eve and George, now fifteen, ran away to the British forces.

Betty Randolph never forgave Eve for leaving. In July 1782, she noted in a codicil to her will, "Eve's bad behavior laid me under the necessity of selling her." Betty's nephew Harrison Randolph apparently bought Eve. He may never have collected his property, however. In a February 1782 newspaper advertisement, he offered a reward "FOR apprehending EVE, Negro woman slave, who left York after the surrender . . . and has since been seen on her way to Hampton." Perhaps Eve managed to hold onto freedom for herself and at least one of her sons.

Ludwell Tenement

Tayloe House

Tayloe Office and Kitchen

upper floor holds the main wind shaft and millstones; the lower floor holds the bolting or sifting apparatus.

The mill requires constant attention to ensure that it faces the wind and that the grinding and bolting operations run properly. If the wind changes direction, the miller lifts the stairs and pushes on the tailpole and wheel to turn the mill to face the wind. Today, visitors to Robertson's Windmill can climb the stairs to see the scene that greeted colonists who brought grain to the miller.

Around the windmill lie fields and pastures planted with corn, wheat, tobacco, and other agricultural products important to Virginia's economy in the eighteenth century. Here, visitors learn about the ■**Rural Trades** familiar to most colonial Virginians. Seasonal farm activities such as cider making and basketmaking are practiced here at various times of the year.

The ■**Cooper** also is located at the windmill. Usually itinerants, coopers who worked in the town of Williamsburg primarily made and repaired buckets, pails, and churns. Outside of town, production sites such as a mill or farm would have needed coopers to construct and repair casks for cider, grain, tobacco, and other products. Staves split from oak are formed into a circle, held in place by trussing hoops, shaped by heat, and finally are given a tight-fitting head. These utilitarian products of the cooper made possible the delivery of Virginia's agricultural bounty.

In contrast to relatively flat and straight Duke of Gloucester Street, Nicholson Street is an undulating lane that moves across a series of hills and valleys and crosses several gullies that run from the high ground of the town toward Queen's Creek and eventually to the York River. Geography affected the desirability of lots along Nicholson Street. The high ground was reserved for the few large estates in the area, leaving the cuts and washes to light industry. For example, the west end of Anthony Hay's cabinetmaking shop is built directly over a stream.

The **Ludwell Tenement,** just to the east of the Peyton Randolph House, reaffirms another characteristic of Williamsburg's back streets: rental property and smaller houses coexisted with the homes of such well-to-do residents as the Randolphs and the Tayloes. In 1770, the Ludwell Tenement was identified as "the Tenement adjoining the Speaker," meaning the rental property next to the dwelling of Peyton Randolph.

The ■**Brickmaker's Yard** is located behind the Tayloe House. The growth of the town in the mid-1770s sustained a concentration of carpenters, joiners, bricklayers, and plasterers. Although bricks were often made at or near building sites, brickyards like this one would have been familiar to eighteenth-century residents.

Built midway into the eighteenth century, the gambrel-roofed **Tayloe House** changed hands in 1759 for six hundred pounds, a very

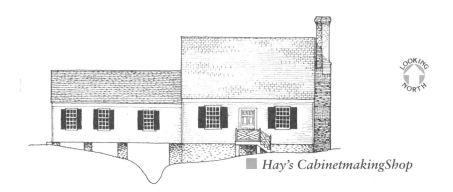

LOOKING NORTH

■ *Hay's CabinetmakingShop*

high price for a frame house at that time. One of the wealthiest men in colonial Virginia, Colonel John Tayloe, owner of the magnificent plantation called Mt. Airy in Richmond County, purchased the building probably for use as a town house. Tayloe served on the Council for many years.

The **Tayloe Office** just east of the house has an interesting "ogee," or bell-shaped, roof. This, too, is an original building.

■**Hay's Cabinetmaking Shop** on the north edge of town occupied low ground between two substantial residences. On this site, a succession of cabinetmakers made some of the finest furniture in the colonies. Like London and other American cabinetmakers, they also repaired furniture and musical instruments, resilvered mirrors, and made exotic "Gothic" garden fences. Williamsburg cabinetmakers also ran an elaborate funeral service that included expensive coffins and hearse rentals. During the Revolution, work-

The master cabinetmaker instructs his assistant, or "journeyman."

■ *Tenant House*

Booker Tenement

men in Hay's shop cleaned and repaired arms for the American forces.

Anthony Hay, who had been a cabinetmaker in Williamsburg for several years, bought this lot in 1756. Hay gave up the business in 1766, when he purchased the Raleigh Tavern, but he and his wife continued to live on the property. Subsequent renters of the shop included cabinetmakers Benjamin Bucktrout (who advertised that he also made and repaired spinets and harpsichords) and Edmund Dickinson (probably Hay's former journeyman). Carver and gilder George Hamilton worked on this site, too.

Archaeologists found the waterlogged remains of a fence rail in the stream bed under the western part of the shop. The seven-foot-long artifact showed both the crude form of the wood rail and the spacing between the pickets that had been nailed to it. The fence in front of the shop faithfully reproduces these details. Archaeological discoveries also provided evidence of clay roofing tiles like those

that now cover the shop.

East of the cabinetmaking shop stands the ■ **Tenant House.** The working class made up almost 25 percent of eighteenth-century Williamsburg's population; this wooden structure is typical of those that housed the town's "lesser sort." At the Tenant House, visitors learn about the people who rented these modest dwellings and sought employment wherever they could find it.

Many of the town's smaller households were located on Williamsburg's back streets. The **Elizabeth Reynolds House** on the south side of Nicholson Street is one of the few structures on the street that faces north.

In 1777, *Virginia Gazette* printer William Hunter deeded a narrow strip of land containing a house and garden to his mother, Elizabeth Reynolds. Hunter was illegitimate, and although his father had acknowledged William in his will, he failed to provide for the boy's mother. Hunter's sense of duty seems to have been greater than his father's. In addition to the house and lot, he agreed

Elizabeth Reynolds House

William Randolph Lodgings

Coke-Garrett House

to pay Elizabeth an annuity of forty pounds and to furnish a "servant maid fit and able to serve wait and attend her."

Just down the street is another example of the contrast in land use so commonplace in eighteenth-century Virginia. An unusually narrow building, the **William Randolph Lodgings** was "letten for Lodgins" in 1735 to William Randolph, the uncle of Peyton Randolph. A burgess and later a councillor, William obviously considered this modest structure an appropriate residence when he came to Williamsburg on government business.

The next building on the north side of Nicholson Street, the small one and one-half story **Booker Tenement,** is typical of a Williamsburg house of the "middling sort." An analysis of the tree growth ring in its timbers showed that the wood was cut about 1823. Documentary evidence indicates that Richard Booker, carpenter and town constable, had begun to rent out rooms in his newly built tenement by the spring of 1826.

■**THE PUBLIC GAOL.** A description of the Public Gaol begins on page 67.

Facing south on Nicholson Street near its intersection with Waller Street is the **Coke-Garrett House.** In 1755, John Coke, a goldsmith and tavern keeper who already owned a house and three lots immediately to the east, bought the two lots on which the story and one-half west section stands. It dates from the eighteenth century. The one and one-

half story east section is an eighteenth-century structure that was moved to this site from an unknown location around 1837. The two-story center portion was built around 1836–1837 during the Garrett family's ownership. The brick office that served as Dr. Robert Garrett's surgery after the battle of Williamsburg in 1862 apparently dates from about 1810. Dr. Garrett treated the wounded of both armies here.

The subdued Greek Revival architecture of the center section merges easily with the colonial styles of the east and west wings. The brick office bears full evidence of the Greek Revival style in its columned and pedimented porch. An interesting feature of the eighteenth-century porch on the west wing, one of the few to have survived in Tidewater Virginia, is its "Chinese Chippendale" porch railing.

Archaeologists found crucibles with traces of gold and silver, a small silver bar, a gold earring, and an engraver's trial piece—all evidence of John Coke's gold- and silversmithing activities—on the site. They also discovered wineglasses, a fine punch bowl, and other artifacts that could be associated with a tavern.

Coke left a personal estate valued at £772 when he died in 1767. His widow, Sarah, continued to operate or rent out the house as a tavern. Her versatile son, Robey, repaired wagons, mounted cannon, and helved axes during the Revolution. The Garrett family acquired the property in 1810; Garretts owned it for well over a century.

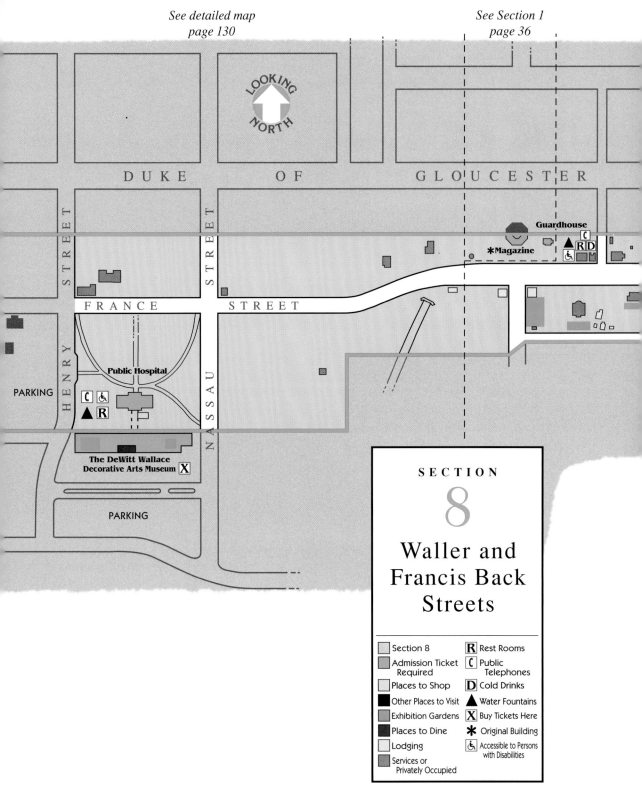

See detailed map
page 130

See Section 1
page 36

LOOKING NORTH

D U K E   O F   G L O U C E S T E R

HENRY STREET

STREET

Guardhouse

✳**Magazine**

C
R D

F R A N C E   S T R E E T

N A S S A U   S T R E E T

Public Hospital

C ♿
▲ R

PARKING

The DeWitt Wallace
Decorative Arts Museum X

PARKING

SECTION

8

Waller and Francis Back Streets

☐ Section 8	**R**	Rest Rooms
☐ Admission Ticket Required	**C**	Public Telephones
☐ Places to Shop	**D**	Cold Drinks
■ Other Places to Visit	▲	Water Fountains
☐ Exhibition Gardens	**X**	Buy Tickets Here
■ Places to Dine	✳	Original Building
☐ Lodging	♿	Accessible to Persons with Disabilities
☐ Services or Privately Occupied		

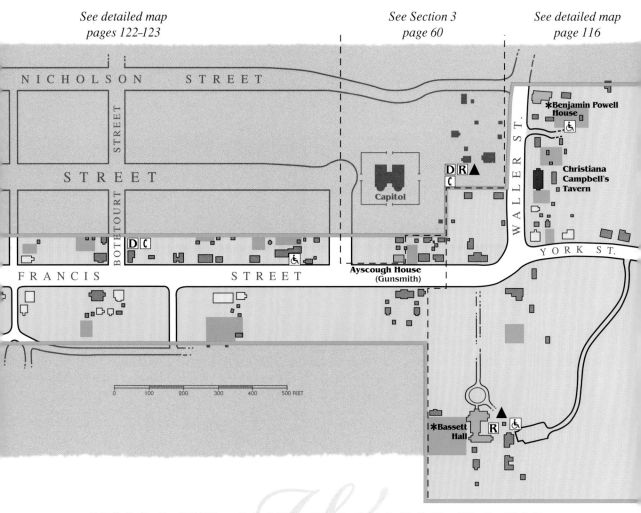

See detailed map
pages 122–123

See Section 3
page 60

See detailed map
page 116

NICHOLSON STREET

STREET

STREET

Capitol

D R
C

Ayscough House
(Gunsmith)

D C

FRANCIS STREET

BOTETOURT STREET

WALLER ST.

*Benjamin Powell
House

Christiana
Campbell's
Tavern

YORK ST.

*Bassett
Hall

R

0 100 200 300 400 500 FEET

WALLER AND FRANCIS BACK STREETS

*An asterisk (*) indicates that a building is an original
eighteenth- or nineteenth-century structure. A ▪ indicates
that you need an admission ticket to see an attraction.*

Early in the eighteenth century, Francis and Waller Streets defined the southern and eastern limits, respectively, of the colonial capital. Town met country on the south side of Williamsburg. Slave quarters, outbuildings, barns, and fields lay immediately beyond Williamsburg's southern boundary. Then the landscape stretched away into broad meadows and wooded hillsides.

The eastern outskirts of town began to change by mid-century. Several recently built lodging houses and taverns catered to transients and townspeople who had business at the nearby Capitol. Williamsburg's second theater became a center of imported British culture, and the racetrack just east of town drew large crowds. As Williamsburg grew, a shortage of residential space in this area spurred the development of subdivisions at the east end of town and along Francis Street. A number of local tradesmen took advantage of the opportunity to buy small lots at attractive prices. An artisan could build a dwelling and perhaps open a shop here.

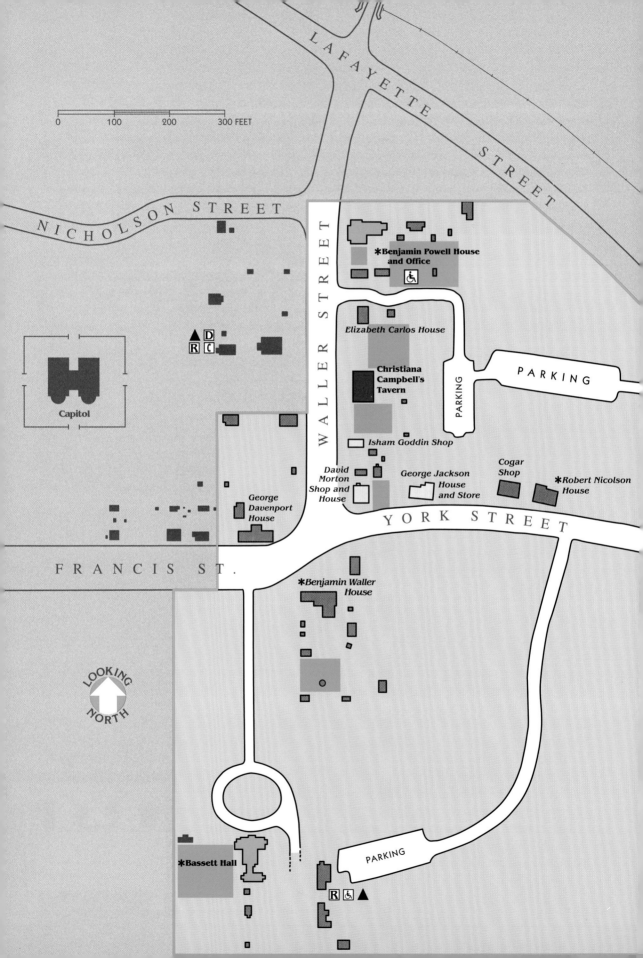

L A F A Y E T T E   S T R E E T

0   100   200   300 FEET

N I C H O L S O N   S T R E E T

WALLER STREET

*Benjamin Powell House and Office

Elizabeth Carlos House

Christiana Campbell's Tavern

PARKING

PARKING

Isham Goddin Shop

Capitol

David Morton Shop and House

George Jackson House and Store

Cogar Shop

*Robert Nicolson House

George Davenport House

Y O R K   S T R E E T

F R A N C I S   S T .

*Benjamin Waller House

LOOKING NORTH

*Bassett Hall

PARKING

R

■*Benjamin Powell House   *Benjamin Powell Office   Elizabeth Carlos House

The ■Benjamin Powell House is named for a successful builder who obtained the property in 1763. A general contractor (or "undertaker," to use the eighteenth-century term), Powell worked on a number of public buildings in Williamsburg. He repaired the Public Gaol in 1764 and 1765, built the tower and steeple at Bruton Parish Church in 1769, and put up the Public Hospital between 1771 and 1773. Along with Peyton Randolph, George Wythe, and other men of similar standing, Powell served on a committee that enforced an embargo of selected British goods in 1774. Today, the Benjamin Powell House is open seasonally to school groups and other visitors.

Powell sold the property in 1782, and it changed hands several times before Benjamin Carter Waller, the son of an early owner,

MEET . . . CATHERINE RATHELL

Catherine Rathell came to Virginia from London in 1765 or 1766 "with a view of setting up a Milliners Shop at Williamsburg." Although she initially settled in Fredericksburg, Mrs. Rathell traveled to the capital during legislative and court sessions to sell goods here. By 1768, she had opened a shop in Williamsburg and was also taking in lodgers. An active businesswoman, Mrs. Rathell went wherever customers could be found. She opened a shop in Annapolis in 1769 and intended to open one in Petersburg in 1772, but she always came back to Williamsburg.

Mrs. Rathell's stock in trade included a variety of fashionable goods imported from London. She sold such items as fabric, lace, fans, ribbons, jewelry, buttons, gloves, shoes, spoons, hats, caps, canes, and riding whips. She was very particular about the quality of her goods, insisting that they be "the very best & most fashionable goods in Williamsburg." When she could, Mrs. Rathell traveled to London to choose merchandise herself. At other times, she ordered through a London merchant house.

In protest against British policies toward the colonies, the Continental Congress passed a resolution in October 1774 forbidding the importation of British goods. Local committees were elected to enforce the boycott. This resolution was disastrous for those whose livelihoods depended on being able to import British products. In April 1775, milliner and merchant Catherine Rathell announced her intention to return to England "till Liberty of Importation is allowed." She boarded the ship *Peggy* and set sail. The ship sank within sight of the port of Liverpool. All of the passengers, including Mrs. Rathell, perished.

bought it in 1794. The small brick building next to the restored house probably served as the office of Waller's son, Dr. Robert Waller, to whom he deeded that part of the property in 1814. The temple-style brick office is similar to the one at the Coke-Garrett House across the street.

Elizabeth Carlos bought the lot on which a story and one-half frame house now stands in 1772. Typical of Williamsburg's more modest dwellings, the dusky brown color of the reconstructed **Elizabeth Carlos House** would have been familiar to early residents, since not every house in town was painted white.

A manuscript account book records purchases of gloves, hose, ribbons, thread, and fabric from Mrs. Carlos in 1777 and indicates that she made aprons and gowns. This evidence suggests that Elizabeth Carlos was a milliner and dressmaker who carried on her business in her home.

Christiana Campbell announced in October 1771 that she had opened a "Tavern in the House, behind the Capitol," where she promised "genteel Accommodations, and the very best Entertainment," by which she meant food and drink. A distinguished clientele patronized Mrs. Campbell's. When George Washington came to town to attend the House of Burgesses in the spring of 1772, he recorded in his diary that he dined there ten times within two months. Washington and his friends often gathered at **Christiana Campbell's Tavern** for refreshments and discussions of everything from horse races to politics.

George Jackson House and Store

Today, dinner at Christiana Campbell's Tavern features specialties such as fried chicken, oyster fritters, crab cakes, Carolina fish muddle, filet mignon, deep-dish vermicelli pie, spoon bread, and sweet potato muffins.

Militiaman Isham Goddin acquired the small **Isham Goddin Shop** in 1778 for two hundred pounds. In 1783, he sold his plot and building for only ninety pounds, a decrease that reflects both wartime inflation and the collapse of Williamsburg property values after the capital moved to Richmond in 1780. The shop now serves as a hotel accommodation.

In 1777, tailor David Morton purchased the lot on the corner of Waller and York Streets for four hundred pounds, a sum that indicates the transaction included the **David Morton House and Shop** and the shop next door, which Morton sold to Isham Goddin the next year. Morton, an active member of the Williamsburg Lodge of Masons, served as treasurer of the lodge from 1780 to 1786. Today, his house is a hotel facility.

The **George Jackson House and Store** on

Christiana Campbell's Tavern

Isham Goddin Shop

Cogar Shop

*Robert Nicolson House

York Street was once owned by a patriotic merchant who risked his life as well as his fortune during the Revolutionary War. Jackson chartered a ship, sailed it to Bermuda, and returned with a supply of much-needed gunpowder for the American forces.

Jackson acquired the property shortly after he moved to Williamsburg from Norfolk in 1773 or 1774. The different roof slopes indicate that this building was, in effect, two buildings. The window and door arrangements of the east wing are typical of shops in the eighteenth century, and the rear chimney would have heated a small counting room. Jackson probably used this part of the structure as his store. The property now serves as hotel accommodations.

The **Cogar Shop**, a small eighteenth-century building, was moved from King and Queen County to this lot in 1947. Colonial Williamsburg later acquired this property.

Robert Nicolson, a tailor and merchant, built the last structure on York Street, the gambrel-roofed **Robert Nicolson House**, about mid-century. The off-center entrance door testifies to two periods of construction, the eastern part possibly as early as 1752 and the western part a little later. For several years thereafter, Nicolson took in lodgers.

Nicolson initially had his shop across the street. When his eldest son, William, joined him in the tailoring business in 1774, they opened a shop and store on Duke of Gloucester Street, a much better location for commercial purposes. During the Revolution, Nicolson served on the local committee of safety. He and William provided uniforms to the American army.

On the south side of Francis Street is the motor vehicle entrance to **Bassett Hall.** Set off by gardens, original outbuildings, and a long, tree-shaded approach, this two-story frame house served for many years as the Williamsburg home of Mr. and Mrs. John D. Rockefeller, Jr. Bassett Hall is closely associated with the restoration of Williamsburg. The Reverend W. A. R. Goodwin, who was instrumental in interesting the philanthropists in restoring Virginia's colonial capital, urged the Rockefellers to select Bassett Hall as their Williamsburg home. Abby Aldrich Rockefeller, a founder of the Museum of Modern Art, furnished the house with examples of American folk art and created a comfortable family atmosphere conducive to relaxation.

The Rockefeller family bequeathed Bassett Hall, its furnishings, and its 585 acres of woodlands to Colonial Williamsburg in 1979. The interior of the house has remained substan-

David Morton Shop and House

Bassett Hall

tially as it appeared when Mr. and Mrs. Rockefeller restored and furnished it in the mid-1930s. Visitors may tour the house and gardens.

The Bassett Hall property is part of a large plot of land that belonged to the Bray family in the seventeenth century. Adjacent to the southern town limits of Williamsburg, this tract joined some 950 acres with four lots in the city, a combination that blurred the lines between town and country.

Benjamin Waller acquired the property on which the **Benjamin Waller House** is located before 1750, and it remained in the Waller family for over a century. A prominent Williamsburg attorney, Waller was George

*Benjamin Waller House

George Davenport House

Wythe's law teacher. He held a variety of offices during an impressive career: burgess, city recorder, judge of the Court of Admiralty, and vestryman of Bruton Parish.

Waller probably used the office, which is adjacent to the house on the east, in his law practice. The smokehouse is an original structure. Behind the Benjamin Waller House is a formal garden open to ticket holders. It has been re-created with the help of a sketch drawn in the early 1800s.

Like most old houses, this house is the product of several building phases. The earliest portion is the single large room to the left of the front door. Later on, a center stair passage and then a large formal room for entertaining were added to the west end, followed by a gambrel-roofed extension in the rear.

The horizontal weatherboards, some of them original, on the dormer cheeks are unusual because such boards are generally attached at an angle that matches the roof slope. The ornamental fence pickets at the east end of the yard are copied from a surviving

eighteenth-century specimen that had been used in reroofing the house during the nineteenth century.

The **George Davenport House** across the street once belonged to attorney George Davenport, whose descendants owned the property until 1779. In 1780, John Draper, a blacksmith who had come to Virginia with Governor Botetourt in 1768, bought the property. Draper operated a blacksmith and farrier business on Duke of Gloucester Street.

In 1765, seventeen local residents received permission from the York County Court "for occasional Worship" at a house "situate on a part of a Lott belonging to Mr. George Davenport as a place for Public Worship of God according to the Practice of Protestant Dissenters of the Presbyterian denomination."

The **James Moir House** and **James Moir Shop** are named for the tailor who owned this property from 1777 to about 1800 and operated his business on the site.

Walker Maury, a 1775 graduate of the College of William and Mary, established a grammar school in the old Capitol in 1784. In an effort to supplement his income, Moir advertised that he had "furnished his house to accommodate eight or ten [pupils] with the greatest degree of conveniency." Moir offered "to lodge, board, wash and mend for them, at a very low price."

■**AYSCOUGH HOUSE.** A description of the Ayscough House is on page 69.

In a letter written in 1809, St. George

■*Bassett Hall*

See Section 1, page 36

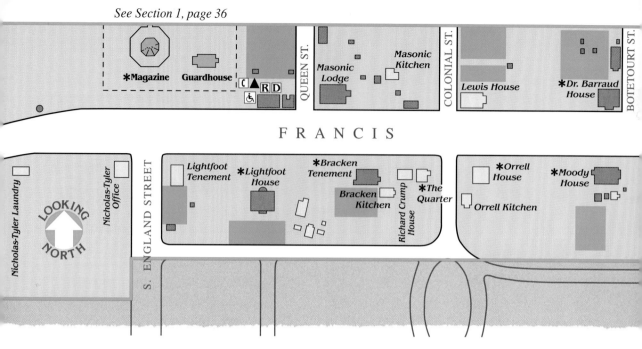

FRANCIS

ℬecoming ᴧmericans
Our Struggle to Be Both Free and Equal

RELIGION IN VIRGINIA

Imagine an age in which religion permeated everyday life and learning; a society in which the law sent people to court if they failed to attend the Church of England and required Quakers, Presbyterians, Baptists, and other non-Anglicans to register with the authorities; a system that empowered parish vestries to tax people of all religions to pay for poor relief, Anglican ministers' salaries, and repairs to Anglican churches such as Bruton Parish Church in Williamsburg. But think also of a clash of cultures in which Native Americans resisted English colonists' attempts at conversion and many slaves learned more than obedience from Christianity.

In the wake of the religious revivals known as the Great Awakening, many Virginians—black and white, rich and poor—sought spiritual renewal among evangelical Presbyterians and Baptists. These "New Lights," as they were called, increasingly ignored legal restraints on dissenters and pressured legislators to abolish Virginia's state church. Meanwhile, "enlightened" views gained from the study of history, philosophy, science, and religion led Thomas Jefferson, James Madison, and other Revolutionary leaders to insist that free exercise of religion be among the rights they would go to war to secure.

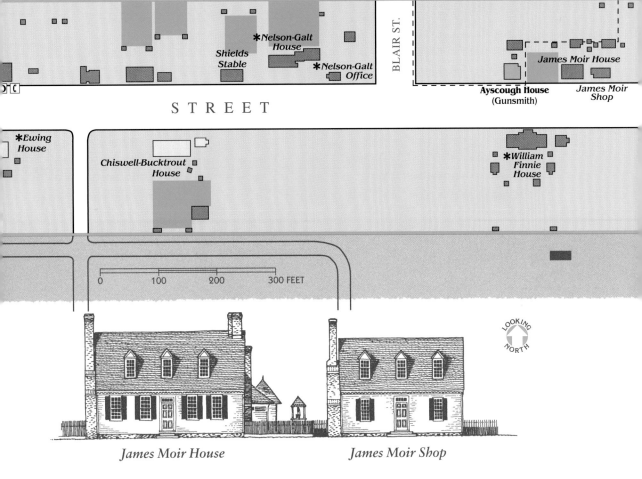

See Section 3, page 60

James Moir House

James Moir Shop

Tucker called the **William Finnie House** on the south side of Francis Street "the handsomest house in town." It is a precursor of the classicism that began to change the American architectural scene after the Revolution.

From the 1770s to the mid-1780s, William Finnie and his family lived here. During the American Revolution, Finnie served as quartermaster general of the Southern Department.

James Semple, a judge and professor of law at the college, acquired the property in 1800 and insured the house and all of its outbuildings for two thousand dollars. A sketch of the front of the building drawn on the insurance declaration documents that the house looked then just as it does today. The William Finnie House is depicted on the Frenchman's Map of 1782. The **William Finnie Quarters**, the

*William Finnie Quarters

*William Finnie House

Shields Stable

*Nelson-Galt House

small building just east of the house, is also an original structure.

In the eighteenth century, several lots—now vacant—along Francis Street combined with property south of the town's boundary to form urban estates. The people who lived here often described their residences as being "pleasantly situated."

The **Nelson-Galt House** on the north side of Francis Street is the oldest dwelling in Williamsburg. It was constructed in 1695. William Robertson, clerk of the Council, bought the property and remodeled the house about 1709.

Thomas Nelson, a member of a prominent Yorktown family, owned the house later in the century. General Nelson, who signed the Declaration of Independence, commanded Virginia's forces during the Yorktown campaign and succeeded Thomas Jefferson as governor of the Commonwealth of Virginia.

Dr. Alexander Dickie Galt, visiting physician at the Public Hospital, purchased the house in 1823. Descendants of the Galt family, residents of Williamsburg since colonial days, continued to live here until recently.

The small **Nelson-Galt Office** nearby is also original. In the eighteenth century, the word "office" described any outbuilding not otherwise designated as to use.

The next structure to the west on Francis Street is an unpainted stable located at the back of the lot belonging to Shields Tavern, which fronts on Duke of Gloucester Street. The rough appearance of **Shields Stable** is probably typical of many backyard outbuildings in colonial Williamsburg.

The elongated hipped-roof line of the **Chiswell-Bucktrout House** is a style unusual in Williamsburg, although it was common in England at the beginning of the eighteenth century. A study of roof timbers and numbered beams in the surviving portions of the largely reconstructed dwelling established the original form of the roof.

In 1766, Colonel John Chiswell became the center of a scandal that "put the whole country into a ferment." Accused of killing Robert Rutledge during a tavern brawl, Colonel Chiswell was arrested for murder. As was customary in such cases, bail was refused, but three of the colonel's friends, who

Chiswell-Bucktrout House

*Nelson-Galt Kitchen and *Office*

were also judges of the General Court, reversed the decision and released Chiswell on bail. The less privileged attributed this unusually lenient procedure to the colonel's political and family connections. The colonel died the day before his trial—by his own hand, it was rumored.

Cabinetmaker Benjamin Bucktrout resided and worked here by the 1770s. Today, the Chiswell-Bucktrout House and Kitchen are hotel facilities.

The **Ewing House** is named for Ebenezer Ewing, a Scottish merchant. When he died in 1795, Ewing left the house to Elizabeth Ashton, the mother of his illegitimate son Thomas, with the proviso that "the moment she marries . . . it becomes the property of my son." Elizabeth remained single until her death four years later, when young Thomas inherited the dwelling. In 1805, the Williamsburg Hustings Court ordered the boy's legal guardian "to bond out Thomas Ewing for three years to learn the art of seaman or mariner"; Thomas disappeared before completing his apprenticeship. The Ewing House and Shop are now hotel accommodations.

Ewing House

MEET . . .
ADAM WATERFORD

The compiler of the 1775 Williamsburg Census noted that blacks accounted for 52 percent of the 1,880 inhabitants in the capital. Most of the city's African-American residents were slaves who performed domestic duties or who worked in their masters' shops or taverns. Almost all the enslaved men, women, and children were illiterate. Further, no slave was permitted to own property. Adam Waterford was part of Williamsburg's small free black population. Waterford, who made his living as a cooper, learned how to read and write.

Waterford's skills were in great demand in Tidewater Virginia. People used casks—firkins, hogsheads, rundlets, and tuns, to name just a few of the different sizes and shapes of barrels—to transport all sorts of goods. Surviving accounts from the 1770s and 1780s indicate that Waterford provided casks for the Palace, the Public Gaol, and the quartermaster general of the Commonwealth of Virginia.

City records show that Waterford paid taxes for two adults, himself and perhaps his wife, in 1769. It is also possible that he owned or hired a slave. Waterford was able to purchase a lot at the southeast edge of the city (behind present-day Providence Hall House of the Williamsburg Inn) on undeveloped land.

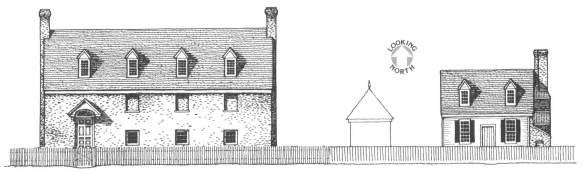

Masonic Lodge

Masonic Kitchen

Josias Moody, a blacksmith, owned the unpretentious house next door from 1794 until he died about 1810. Architectural evidence suggests that the **Moody House** dates from 1725 to 1750. The house was altered several times before reaching its present size and appearance by 1782. The long lean-to roof on the back indicates that additions were made to an earlier structure. The kitchen behind the house is now a hotel facility.

The **Dr. Barraud House** on the northwest corner of Francis and Botetourt Streets was erected before 1782 and incorporated an earlier building on the site. Dr. Philip Barraud, the buyer in 1786, was born in Virginia, saw active service during the Revolution, studied medicine at the University of Edinburgh, and, with Dr. John Minson Galt, served as visiting physician to the Public Hospital until he moved to Norfolk in 1799.

The Dr. Barraud House is one of the few residences that front Francis Street on the north. For the most part, the north side of Francis Street gives access to the back of Duke of Gloucester Street lots, where stables, privies, and other outbuildings were usually located in the eighteenth century.

The **Lewis House** is named for Charles Lewis, who owned the property until 1806 and is believed to have built the original house. Initially the lot was part of the Orlando Jones property, which extended from Duke of Gloucester Street to Francis Street. Hotel guests can now stay in the house.

Probably built between 1750 and 1775, the **Orrell House** takes its name from John Orrell, who acquired the property about 1810.

The entrance hall, or "passage," of the house, an otherwise typical gambrel-roofed dwelling, is not centered, so all of the living quarters are to one side of the passage. The house forms on plan an exact square whose sides measure twenty-eight feet, and, because the roof ridge is twenty-eight feet above the top of the basement wall, it is proportioned as an ideal geometric cube. Today, it is a hotel facility. Colonial Houses guests register for their stay at the nearby Orrell Kitchen.

The Quarter, a small nineteenth-century cottage, is believed to have served for a time

*Moody House

*Orrell House

Lewis House

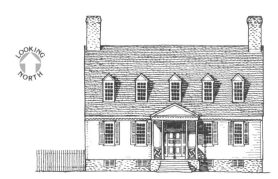

*Dr. Barraud House

as slave quarters. The addition of a shed portion at the rear of the building has resulted in an unusual and attractive roof line. The Quarter is now a hotel facility.

The **Richard Crump House** is named for its late eighteenth-century owner. The Reverend Mr. John Bracken, who had extensive real estate holdings along Francis Street, owned the house briefly along with the **Bracken Tenement** to the west and the **Bracken Kitchen,** which is located between the two dwellings. Hotel guests can stay in the Richard Crump House or the Bracken Kitchen.

Bracken's rise to social and financial prominence began in 1776 with his marriage to Sally Burwell of Carter's Grove plantation. He was the rector of Bruton Parish Church for forty-five years, mayor of Williamsburg in 1796, and president of the College of William and Mary from 1812 to 1814.

As the rector grew older, he grew rotund and perhaps overfond of the grape. In 1815, one observer recounted how Bracken kept a couple waiting at the altar. Apparently the "Round Bellied Vicar" imbibed a drop too

much en route to Yorktown to conduct the wedding. He lost his way, "upset the jigg and broke it," and arrived—wet and muddy—an hour late for the ceremony.

The one and one-half story Bracken Tenement has a steep A-shaped gable roof and massive T-shaped chimneys, each characteristic of early eighteenth-century architecture in Virginia.

The **Masonic Kitchen and Masonic Lodge** on the north side of Francis Street stand where "the ancient and loyal society of free and accepted Masons" met in the late eighteenth century. The Williamsburg chapter, which had been meeting at local taverns since mid-century, received a new charter in 1773. Its members included Peyton Randolph, Peter Pelham, Bishop James Madison, St. George Tucker, and James Monroe.

In the 1770s, the lodge held its regular meetings at Market Square Tavern and patronized Christiana Campbell's for balls and special entertainments. The Masons leased a portion of this lot and met in a building on this property from the 1780s onward. Today,

*The Quarter   *Richard Crump House*   *Bracken Kitchen*   **Bracken Tenement*

The handsome brick Lightfoot House provides accommodations for VIP visitors to Williamsburg. The style of the "Chinese Chippendale" front fence was fashionable about 1750.

the Masonic Kitchen is a hotel facility.

Architectural evidence suggests that the **Lightfoot House,** built about 1730, was brought to its final form in the 1750s. This fine brick residence is unusual in having a second floor as high as the first. It is adorned by a stringcourse in molded brick and by a wrought-iron balcony suggestive of the one at the Palace. The decorative front fence shows the Chinese, or "chinoiserie," influence so popular about 1750.

The Lightfoot family owned this property during much of the eighteenth century. In 1783, Philip Lightfoot advertised the house for sale, describing it as "a large two story brick dwelling house, with four rooms on a floor; its situation is esteemed one of the most pleasant in the City, lying on the back-street near the market." The Reverend John Bracken bought the property in 1786.

The Lightfoot House has been furnished with fine antiques and is equipped with modern conveniences in order to serve as an appropriate guesthouse for distinguished visitors to Williamsburg. The laundry and kitchen

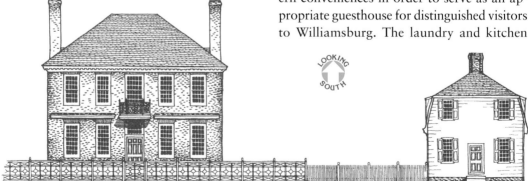

*Lightfoot House

Lightfoot Tenement

The Lightfoot Tenement garden

behind it serve as hotel accommodations.

The Reverend Bracken also bought the **Lightfoot Tenement** next door. In the eighteenth century, the term "tenement" meant simply a rented house. The Lightfoot Tenement is now a hotel facility.

All that remains on the site of the **Nicholas-Tyler House** on the southwest corner of South England Street are two buildings. The **Nicholas-Tyler Office** and **Nicholas-Tyler Laundry** have been reconstructed on their original foundations. The structures are hotel accommodations.

Robert Carter Nicholas bought the prop-erty in 1770 and built a large frame house with numerous outbuildings. Nicholas served as treasurer of the colony of Virginia and later as a judge of the Chancery Court.

A later owner was John Tyler, tenth president of the United States. Tyler and his family were living here when two horsemen reined up in front of the house early on April 5, 1841. They knocked on the door and waited. John Tyler, clad in a nightshirt and cap, finally opened the door, only to learn that President William Henry Harrison had died and the awesome duties of the presidency now rested on his shoulders.

Nicholas-Tyler Office

Nicholas-Tyler Laundry

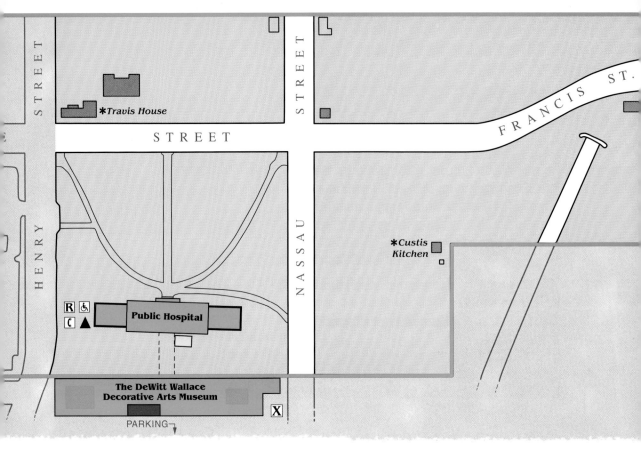

FRANCIS STREET BECOMES FRANCE STREET

In the eighteenth century, the steep sides and muddy bottom of the ravine just ahead separated Francis Street on the east from France Street. Today they form a thorough-fare, with only a dip and curve to mark the end of one and the beginning of the other.

Standing alone on the south side of the street is the **Custis Kitchen.** It marks the eight lots owned by Colonel John Custis—scholar, planter, and eccentric—who settled in Williamsburg about 1715.

*Custis Kitchen

Here Custis built a substantial brick house and a number of outbuildings and cultivated his celebrated garden, one of the most ambi-tious ornamental and experimental gardens in early America. Correspondence that records Custis's exchange of plant specimens with the great English natural history enthusiast, Peter Collinson, has been helpful in planting the gardens of Williamsburg.

When Custis died in 1749, his son, Daniel Parke Custis, inherited Custis Square. Daniel's widow, Martha, subsequently married George Washington, who administered the property until his stepson, John Parke ("Jacky") Custis, came of age in 1778.

Francis Fauquier, one of the colony's most popular royal governors, first proposed the establishment of the ■**Public Hospital** to the House of Burgesses in 1766. Until that time, the insane in Virginia were cared for at home, maintained in a neighbor's house in exchange for money from tax revenues collected by church vestries for poor relief, or confined with vagrants in parish workhouses. Some were even incarcerated in the Williamsburg Public Gaol.

The General Assembly enacted legislation "to make Provision for the support and maintenance of idiots, lunatics, and other persons of unsound Minds" in 1770. The Public Hospital, the first public institution in British North America devoted exclusively to the care and treatment of the mentally ill, opened in 1773. Well-known Philadelphia architect Robert Smith designed the building. George Wythe, John Blair, and Thomas Nelson were among its original trustees.

The Public Hospital continued to minister to the mentally ill of the Commonwealth of Virginia until a disastrous fire swept the facility in 1885 and destroyed the colonial building. The hospital was rebuilt on this site, where it remained until Eastern State Hospital on the outskirts of Williamsburg opened in the mid-1960s.

The Public Hospital was the last major public building of eighteenth-century Williamsburg to be reconstructed. The reconstruction follows the form and details of the original building, which were determined by archaeological investigations and historical research. Exhibits show how the treatment of mental illness evolved in the eighteenth and nineteenth centuries. An underground concourse connects the hospital with the contemporary, two-level DeWitt Wallace Decorative Arts Museum.

Travis House

■ **THE DEWITT WALLACE DECORATIVE ARTS MUSEUM.** A description of The DeWitt Wallace Decorative Arts Museum begins on page 135. The Museum is entered through the Public Hospital.

On the north side of France Street is the **Travis House,** a long, gambrel-roofed frame structure. Colonel Edward Champion Travis, a member of the House of Burgesses, erected the western portion of this dwelling before 1765; later residents added on to the house over the next half-century until it reached its present seventy-foot length. The additions are marked today by the vertical boards that originally were the corner boards of their respective sections. The superintendents of the Public Hospital lived in the Travis House until early in this century.

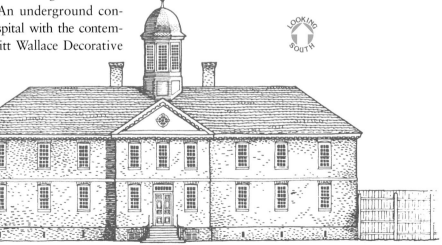

■ *Public Hospital*

■PUBLIC HOSPITAL

"Every civilized Country has an Hospital for these People, where they are confined, maintained and attended by able Physicians, to endeavour to restore to them their lost reason."

Governor Francis Fauquier presented this rationale in 1766 when he first proposed that a hospital be founded to care "for these miserable Objects, who cannot help themselves." On June 4, 1770, the House of Burgesses passed a bill to establish the Public Hospital, which opened in the fall of 1773 as the first public institution in the British North American colonies devoted solely to the care and treatment of the mentally ill.

Over the next eleven decades, the Public Hospital grew into a complex of nine buildings. As the physical appearance of the hospital changed, so too did the ways in which mental illness was regarded and treated.

During the period 1773–1835, the hospital was part prison, part infirmary. Its first keeper, James Galt, had formerly been in charge of the Public Gaol. His wife, Mary,

The interior of a patient's room or cell as it would have appeared in the Public Hospital during the late eighteenth century

became the matron for the female patients. Dr. John de Sequeyra, a physician educated in Holland, served as the attending doctor from 1773 to 1795. He saw patients when they were admitted and once a week thereafter. A court of directors drawn from Virginia's gentry class determined admissions, ordered discharges, and made policy decisions. Only persons considered dangerous or curable were admitted.

Physicians in this "Age of Restraint" regarded mental illness as a disease of the brain, and the belief that mentally disturbed persons could be cured by using scientific knowledge was relatively new. To calm or cure patients, the staff applied mechanical restraints, prescribed potent drugs, employed the ducking chair or plunge bath, and used instruments to bleed them.

The "Moral Management Era," 1836–1862, saw a new approach to mental health care. Moral management deemphasized restraints and stressed the importance of kindness in efforts to cure the mentally ill. Physical labor, organized leisure time activities, and careful medical supervision were also important aspects of everyday life in the Public Hospital during this period. Patients were urged to participate in crafts, gardening, and musical diversions and to talk with one another and with the staff.

The hospital's physical facilities and patient population grew dramatically by the mid-nineteenth century. A third floor was added to the original structure and other buildings were enlarged. By 1859, the hospital housed three hundred patients in seven buildings.

Although the hospital had grown in size by the late nineteenth century, the percentage of patients successfully treated declined drastically. The staff lost confidence in their ability to cure mental illness, and, without a clear sense of direction, the facility became a long-term home for the chronically ill. The Public Hospital had entered its third phase, the "Custodial Care Regime," 1862–1885.

Physical restraints appeared, and a maintenance program of passive diversions such as magic lantern shows, fishing excursions, picnics, and tea parties was instituted. The number of patients rose to more than 440 by 1883, and it became clear that the authorities had decided simply to care for the mentally disturbed without initiating a course of treatment that might result in a cure.

On the night of June 7, 1885, a fire of undetermined origin completely destroyed the eighteenth-century Public Hospital building, which was reconstructed by the Colonial Williamsburg Foundation in 1985.

The exhibit in the east wing of the reconstructed Public Hospital has two parts. From the central hall visitors enter the east passage, a reconstructed historical space that contained six cells (of the total of twenty-four) found in the original building. On the north side of the passage is a central viewing room. From this modern vantage point visitors can look into a re-created eighteenth-century cell, a cold and spare prisonlike interior with chains on the wall and bars at the window. Opposite is a mid-nineteenth-century apartment, a more comfortable environment in which patients were encouraged to communicate with other patients and with the staff. The exhibition cells contrast the treatments and doctor-patient relationships followed in the eighteenth century with those that became popular in the nineteenth century.

Visitors then cross the passage and enter the exhibition area on the south side of the building. This modern space contains a three-part exhibit that graphically shows the different theories about mental illness and methods of treating it that were in fashion from the opening of the Public Hospital until the devastating fire in 1885.

The completion of the Public Hospital, eighteenth-century Williamsburg's last major public building to be reconstructed, adds an important dimension to the presentation and interpretation of everyday life in Virginia's colonial capital.

The interior of a patient's apartment as it would have appeared at the Williamsburg asylum during the mid-1840s

■THE DEWITT WALLACE DECORATIVE ARTS MUSEUM

The DeWitt Wallace Decorative Arts Museum is a bi-level contemporary museum contained within a high brick wall immediately behind the reconstructed Public Hospital. The museum is entered through the hospital lobby at the lower level. Completed in 1985 with funds provided by the late DeWitt Wallace, founder of *Reader's Digest*, the museum contains 62,000 square feet, 27,200 of which is devoted to the exhibition and interpretation of a broad range of primarily British and American decorative arts.

Philadelphia chest on chest

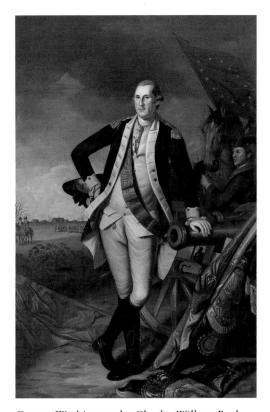

George Washington *by Charles Willson Peale*

Dating from the seventeenth century to the early nineteenth century, these examples include furniture, ceramics, silver and base metals, paintings, prints, textiles and costumes, and many other domestic objects from the Colonial Williamsburg collections.

Designed by the internationally honored architect Kevin Roche, the museum is contemporary in concept and versatile in both function and presentation. The main floor is penetrated by two symmetrically positioned glass-roofed garden courts that allow controlled sunlight to illuminate the adjacent galleries.

The Wallace Museum's rich collections are featured in innovative exhibitions.

A handsome stairway draws visitors through the lower-level Introductory Gallery and leads them up to the main, or ground, level, where the primary exhibition areas are located.

Several different gallery spaces occupy the main level. They include individual media study galleries and galleries for special exhibitions. An array of objects that are important both historically and aesthetically to the study of the colonial period are displayed around the balcony that overlooks the garden court.

Exhibition space on either side of the center area is devoted to a series of study galleries where British and American textiles, maps and prints, metals, and ceramics are permanently displayed. Furniture is exhibited in the Elizabeth Ridgely and Miodrag Blagojevich Furniture Gallery. In these more intimate

spaces, museum visitors can quietly study and absorb subtle differences in styles and techniques as they view greater quantities of objects that span a broader range of aesthetic and technical accomplishment.

The remaining third of the exhibition area, located at the east end of the main level and surrounding a restful skylit court, is devoted to special exhibitions drawn from Colonial Williamsburg's holdings and other sources.

In a wide variety of ways, the objects in these galleries—some of which probably might not have come to Williamsburg because of a variety of factors—help visitors better understand how colonial Virginians, many of whom were transplanted Englishmen and women or their descendants, became Americans. With advance notice, guided tours of the DeWitt Wallace Decorative Arts Museum are offered to complement and enhance visitors' experiences in the Historic Area.

Special lectures, musical events, craft programs, and video presentations are offered (according to a published schedule) in a 240-seat auditorium named for June S. and Joseph H. Hennage. Decorative arts publications as well as reproductions of some of the objects exhibited in the gallery may be purchased in the museum shop adjoining the lower lobby. Luncheon, tea, and other light refreshments are available in the museum's café on the lower level beside the central court.

The superb tall case clock has works by Thomas Tompion.

The Lila Acheson Wallace Garden is a formal, enclosed garden that visitors may enter from the main floor of the Wallace Museum. Opened in 1986, the garden honors Lila Acheson Wallace, who, with her husband, DeWitt Wallace, founded *Reader's Digest.*

British landscape architect Sir Peter Shepheard designed this contemporary garden as a classical space within an open-air courtyard. The garden is appointed with distinctive bronze furniture and relief-molded stoneware pots designed for the Wallace Museum by a well-known team of French sculptors, Claude and François-Xavier LaLanne. Its long, narrow, reflecting pool, which is fitted with bronze bird fountains at the corners, creates the primary vista in the garden and serves as a mirror for a half-size gilt statue of *Diana.* The figure was made in 1985 from a mold of Augustus Saint-Gaudens's original cast, which stood atop the dome of Madison Square Garden in New York City from 1893 to 1925.

The Lila Acheson Wallace Garden features a luxuriant mix of tropical, semitropical, and hardy perennial plantings. Its perennial borders provide color from May to November and are augmented by a collection of container plants that create an inviting space beneath a tall pergola. A hedge of yaupon holly frames the west end of the garden and provides a terminus for the pool, which is planted with water lilies, aquatic cannas, and native iris.

The Lila Acheson Wallace Garden

■ABBY ALDRICH ROCKEFELLER FOLK ART MUSEUM

American folk art is the product of talented but minimally trained or untrained artists and craftspeople working outside the mainstream of academic art. Since colonial times, America's untutored artists have recorded aspects of everyday life, making novel and effective use of whatever media were at hand. Bold colors, simplified shapes, imaginative surface patterns, and the artist's highly original and unself-conscious use of various media are characteristics of the best objects created by amateurs and artisans.

Among the objects on view at the Abby Aldrich Rockefeller Folk Art Museum are pictures done in oil, watercolor, ink, and needlework that describe a variety of subjects, such as portraits, land- and seascapes, scenes of daily life, biblical, historical, and literary pieces, still lifes, fraktur, and family records. Three-dimensional carvings or sculpture executed in wood and metal include weather vanes and wind toys, ship carvings, shop signs, toys, and decoys. Among household furnishings are boxes, woven and quilted bed coverings, pottery, tinware, iron utensils, and furniture embellished with painted decoration. Objects date from the eighteenth century to the present.

The Old Plantation *by an unidentified artist*

Baby in Red Chair *by an unidentified artist*

Abby Aldrich Rockefeller pioneered in collecting American folk art in the late 1920s at a time when others ignored its aesthetic appeal and often considered the material curious, quaint, or worth saving only because of its historical associations. Mrs. Rockefeller sought out and acquired more than 400 pieces of folk art during a ten-year period. In 1935, she loaned the principal part of her collection to Colonial Williamsburg, and in 1939, the loan became a gift. A folk art museum, built in her memory by her husband, John D. Rockefeller, Jr., opened to the public in 1957. Since then, the collection has expanded to more than 2,500 objects. In 1988–1991, the museum facility was enlarged to provide additional exhibition and work space for the Museum's growing visitation and increased programming.

The Folk Art Museum offers changing exhibitions of American folk art from its permanent holdings and sponsors major loan shows. The Museum houses extensive research materials, a library, and a gift shop.

Bactrian camel, watermelon, and barberpole, all of carved and painted wood

Chest of drawers by an unidentified Pennsylvania artist

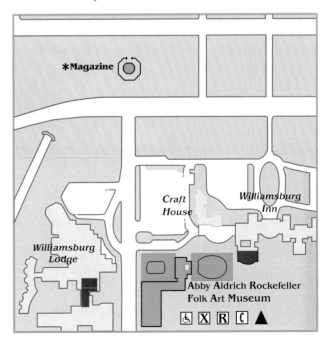

The Country Road links Carter's Grove plantation with Williamsburg. Reminiscent of the roads that linked many riverside plantations in the eighteenth century, the Country Road traverses marshes and tidal creeks and winds through woodlands. It terminates just south of Williamsburg.

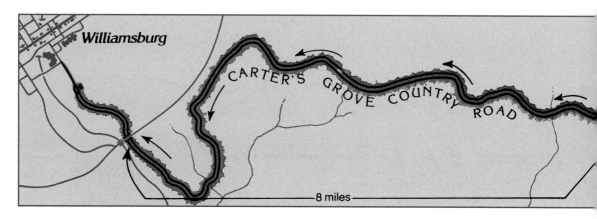

■ CARTER'S GROVE

Six miles southeast of Colonial Williamsburg's Historic Area lies Carter's Grove, whose acres of woods and fields bordering the James River contrast with the urban landscape of the restored city. The histories of the diverse peoples who lived on the land that came to be known as Carter's Grove supplement our knowledge of the eighteenth-century capital. Their experiences help us better understand four centuries of life in Virginia.

The diverse cultural traditions of the peoples who occupied this land are explained in the exhibits and multi-image slide presentation at the Reception Center. For hundreds of years, Native Americans laid claim to this region. By the early seventeenth century, Algonquian settlements were scattered throughout the Chesapeake. The English adventurers who came in pursuit of profit initially coexisted with the tribes but were unprepared for the unfamiliar natives and for the realities of disease and starvation. In time, Africans were brought here to work as laborers and craftsmen. They struggled under the system of slavery but nevertheless preserved much of their communal heritage. Late in the seventeenth century, the small group that made up the gentry class emerged. With the acquisition of sizable acreage, they established domains that symbolized their power and success. The gentry dominated colonial society until the American Revolution.

In the seventeenth century, the Carter's Grove acreage was part of a much larger settlement known as Martin's Hundred. Established by a company of English investors by 1620, two patents granted the proprietors a total of 21,500 acres. A Native American uprising occurred throughout eastern Virginia in March 1622. Many of the inhabitants of

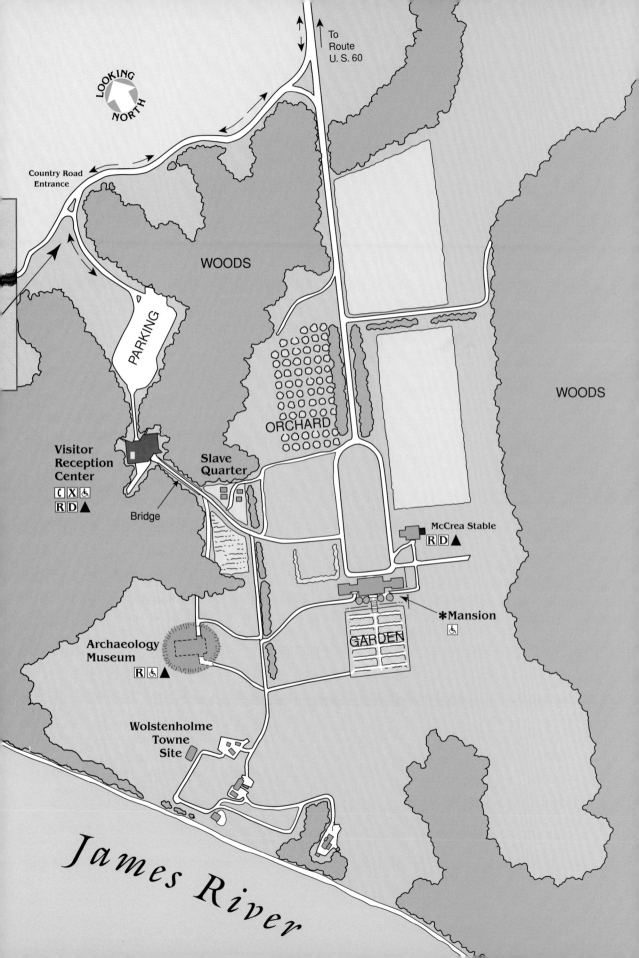

LOOKING NORTH

To Route U.S. 60

Country Road Entrance

WOODS

PARKING

ORCHARD

WOODS

Visitor Reception Center

C X ♿
R D ▲

Slave Quarter

Bridge

McCrea Stable
R D ▲

✱Mansion
♿

GARDEN

Archaeology Museum
R ♿ ▲

Wolstenholme Towne Site

James River

■*Carter's Grove*

Martin's Hundred were killed or captured. Despite attempts to rebuild the settlement, all physical evidence of Martin's Hundred, corrupted to "Merchant's Hundred" in later years, and its principal center, Wolstenholme Towne, had disappeared by 1700.

Robert "King" Carter, the progenitor of a wealthy and influential Virginia family, purchased a 1,400-acre tract of this land for his eldest daughter, Elizabeth, early in the eighteenth century. "King" Carter requested in his will that this property should "in all times to come be called . . . by the name of Carter's Grove." Upon Elizabeth's death, the estate passed to her second son, Carter Burwell.

Carter Burwell lived at Carter's Grove eighteen years, dying six months after the mansion house was completed in 1756. His son, Nathaniel, inherited the estate. When he came of age in 1771, Nathaniel Burwell moved to the plantation. Two decades later, Burwell and his family, like many of their contemporaries, relocated to the western part of Virginia, and Carter's Grove was left in the hands of overseers. Although Carter Burwell III, Nathaniel's oldest son, was born and died here, he may actually have spent little time at Carter's Grove. Philip Lewis Carter Burwell sold the plantation out of the family in 1838, thus ending five generations of ownership by Burwells.

This sale was the first of many to occur in the changing political and economic climate of the nineteenth and twentieth centuries. The estate changed hands nine times between the first transfer and 1900. Three more owners and an unknown number of tenants lived at Carter's Grove before Mr. and Mrs. Archibald McCrea purchased the property in 1928. They were the last individuals to reside here until Colonial Williamsburg received the estate by deed of gift in 1969.

For many residents and visitors of the past and present, the Georgian mansion erected by Carter Burwell has been Carter's Grove most prominent feature. Between 1750 and 1755, Burwell contracted with a number of craftsmen, among them David Minitree, a Williamsburg brickmason, and Richard Baylis, an English carver, to build the main house. Surviving documentary records and account books contain no references to indicate that an architect assisted in the construction of the edifice. Burwell would have consulted architectural handbooks such as *Palladio Londinensis, or the London Art of Building*, for the appropriate ornamentation and details, however. The mansion's superb brickwork, fine woodwork, and sophisticated floor plan are still highly regarded today.

Managing the land that surrounded the mansion was the focus of Nathaniel Burwell's efforts. Although cultivated and cured on his other plantations, tobacco was not grown at Carter's Grove. Instead, meat and dairy products were among the cash crops. Then as now, corn, wheat, and apple orchards covered a portion of the land. Black slaves, some of them craftsmen, composed Nathaniel Burwell's work force and supplied the needs of the agricultural operations of the property.

Although farming continued at "Grove Farm" in the nineteenth century, the various occupants altered the grounds and architecture of the great house to suit their tastes. In 1840 and again in 1868, following the Civil War, a wharf was erected to facilitate transportation and communication with nearby communities. The planting of tulip poplars and other trees enhanced the property. Red-, white-, and blue-painted woodwork and a long veranda were among the modifications to the mansion in the late 1800s.

The most influential restyling of Carter's Grove occurred after the McCreas acquired it. Virginia architect Duncan Lee, who had previously contributed to an expansion of the governor's residence in Richmond, directed their renovation of the mansion.

MEET . . . WILLIAM MOODY, JR.

In addition to Carter's Grove plantation, Carter Burwell and his son Nathaniel owned several plantations, or "quarters," as they were called in the eighteenth century. In 1764, William Moody, Jr., began working for the Burwells as an overseer at Fouaces Quarter in nearby York County. Moody supervised the eight field hands that Burwell owned and had assigned to Fouaces. The overseer was responsible for most aspects of the day-to-day management of the farm. He had to know when to plant and when to harvest and how to get the most from every field hand and every acre.

Tobacco was the main crop at Fouaces. Wheat, corn, cider, pork, beef, mutton, wool, milk, and butter also brought in income. In lieu of a salary, Moody received two and one-half shares of the produce of the farm, an incentive for him to make the agricultural operations at Fouaces efficient and productive.

Sometimes an overseer was allowed to grow his own tobacco crop on his employer's land. Since Moody owned at least five slaves, he probably put them to work in his plot of tobacco. Like many other young overseers, Moody hoped to accumulate enough capital to acquire a farm of his own.

By 1750, four generations of Moodys had lived in York County for more than a century. They were hard working, well respected, civic-minded people. Moody family members often served on juries and as estate appraisers.

In 1772, Moody married "Barbary," the widow of his friend Frederick Bryan, for whose will Moody had acted as executor. Shortly thereafter, Moody bought 175 acres of land in York County, to which he soon added 150 more that he acquired from Burwell. By the late 1770s, Moody had managed to establish himself as a landowning planter in his own right.

The roof ridge of the main house, originally a two-story structure, was raised, and dormer windows were installed to accommodate the addition of a third floor. The riverfront walls of the mansion's flanking outbuildings, the kitchen to the east and the laundry to the west, which are believed to predate the house, were remodeled accordingly. Despite these alterations, the original roofline was retained and remains visible among the bricks in the west wall of the western dependency. Two sections, or hyphens, were erected to connect the three eighteenth-century buildings. Modern improvements such as heating, plumbing, and electricity were added.

Impressive changes to the grounds accompanied the revival of the house. Boxwood gardens were planted on the north side of the mansion. Landscape architect Arthur Shurcliff, who also led the reshaping of Colonial Williamsburg's landscape, opened the magnificent vista to the river. To impress visitors who arrived at Carter's Grove by automobile, Shurcliff chose to emphasize the land approach. In the eighteenth century, by contrast, the more formal facade and the more elaborately carved and paneled rooms faced the water.

Guided by Lee and Shurcliff, the McCreas transformed—and in a sense reclaimed—the colonial past out of which Carter's Grove was born. In a changing modern world, they looked back to re-create an idealized Virginia plantation and to preserve the values embodied in that vision.

Following tradition, Carter's Grove continued to function as a working farm during the McCreas' tenure. Turkeys, chickens, and cows roamed the grounds. Black servants supplied essential support for the day-to-day operations of the plantation. The mansion became a place of grandeur, one that would have equaled the original stature of the house in the eighteenth century. Mrs. McCrea entertained here often until her death in 1960.

The wish she shared with her husband, to have subsequent generations enjoy the house and grounds, was realized when the Sealantic Charitable Trust, a Rockefeller family philanthropic organization, purchased the estate for the Colonial Williamsburg Foundation in 1963. For the next several years, in keeping with the focus of the Historic Area, eighteenth-century plantation life was the primary theme of the interpretation. This perspective began to change in the 1980s, however.

Archaeological research that began in 1970 provided the impetus for this new thinking. By the end of the next year, remains that suggested earlier occupation of the land had been found. In addition, archaeologists uncovered evidence of an eighteenth-century garden at the base of the mansion's terraced slopes. This early garden, with its numerous paths, had been enclosed by a fence, a feature that is reflected in its presentation today. Carter or Nathaniel Burwell likely viewed a garden of vegetables, herbs, and flowers from the mansion during his tenure on the property.

The structures that lie between the mansion and the river today tell the story of Martin's Hundred. With partial support from the National Geographic Society, archaeologists searched for clues of this settlement between 1976 and 1982. Since that time, efforts to identify and interpret the Martin's Hundred artifacts and layers of soil have culminated in the opening of the Winthrop Rockefeller Archaeology Museum in 1991.

Designed by Kevin Roche, the architect of the Public Hospital and the DeWitt Wallace Decorative Arts Museum, the museum is nestled under a knoll southeast of the mansion. Inside, excavation photographs and parts of weapons, agricultural tools, ceramics, and domestic artifacts describe the settlers' homeland in the Old World and their strategies for survival in the New World. Paintings, docu-ments, and audiovisual exhibits explain how archaeologists assess their discoveries. Two helmets, the first intact close helmets found in North America, are displayed outside the entrance to a small theater where the film *The Wolstenholme Treasure* recounts their recovery and preservation.

Beyond the museum's exit stands a schematic interpretation of part of the settlement, which includes the Wolstenholme Towne fort, store, barn, and domestic unit. Barrel-housed stations offer explanations that relate the archaeological findings to the partial re-creation. A partial reconstruction of the site, believed to have been occupied by Martin's Hundred settler John Boys, is located along the river to the east.

The reconstructed slave quarter represents material life as it was lived by the vast majority of the inhabitants of the Chesapeake—both black and white. Two double houses, a corn crib, a single family dwelling, small garden plots, and chicken pens positioned around a courtyard represent a small community.

Forebears of some of the Carter's Grove slaves had lived in the area since the 1660s. Others came from present-day eastern Nigeria or western Cameroon in the 1720s. By the mid-eighteenth century, many had ties to several hundred other slaves living on Burwell family farms in the neighborhood. These individuals selectively adapted elements from their mixed African and Virginian heritage to create a unique African-American culture. Current interpretation stresses the richness and complexity of that culture and discusses the few material goods that most slaves possessed.

The stability of the slave community at Carter's Grove depended on the profitability of tobacco agriculture in the Tidewater. When, in the last quarter of the eighteenth century, the Burwells decided their future was on the frontier, most of the slaves were forced to move to western Virginia.

The land that defines Carter's Grove, its most enduring asset, links the generations of those who lived there. Agricultural endeavors, which supported many of these peoples, are appropriately a part of the interpretive story. Oats and rye are sown in the fields, and animals that are part of Colonial Williamsburg's rare breed conservation program forage on the grounds.

Just as the landscape of Carter's Grove has changed in the last decade, so, too, has the mansion's interior. The McCreas' assortment of seventeenth- to twenty-first-century furnishings again fill the house, just as they did in the 1930s. The room arrangements replicate the known use of space in the eighteenth century, with the kitchen wing allocated to servants, the centralized formal areas designated for visitors, and the more comfortable, private retreats reserved for the family. The presentation of the mansion house today thus preserves the significant efforts of the McCreas during the Colonial Revival period and brings the history of Carter's Grove full circle to the twenty-first century.

Carter's Grove is reached by Route 60 East. A country road (one way) runs between the Reception Center and the Historic Area.

Clockwise from upper left: *Wolstenholme Towne, two rare helmets excavated at Carter's Grove, the slave quarter*

DINING

From colonial sippets to Continental cuisine, you'll satisfy your appetite at Colonial Williamsburg.

Dine in one of our eighteenth-century taverns—Chowning's Tavern, Christiana Campbell's Tavern, the King's Arms Tavern, or Shields Tavern—where you can enjoy dishes inspired by early American recipes. Colonial politicians, the elite, and travelers gathered at taverns to partake of hearty meals, spirits, gossip, and music. Today, this atmosphere of

Dine by candlelight at the King's Arms Tavern.

mirth, song, and tempting aromas still prevails with costumed servers in authentically re-created dining rooms and conversation that competes with the rollicking songs of strolling balladeers. Eat at a colonial tavern for one of the most memorable dining experiences you'll ever have.

Our contemporary restaurants are equally distinctive. The award-winning Regency Room at the Williamsburg Inn offers unparalleled cuisine, elegance, and service. If you're looking for scrumptious food in a more casual atmosphere, try the Williamsburg Lodge Bay Room, the Lodge Café, or the Golden Horseshoe Clubhouses. Sample contemporary favorites at Huzzah!, the all-new, family-style restaurant adjacent to the Woodlands Hotel & Suites.

What are sippets? Toasted pieces of bread you dip into soup. Once you try them, you may never go back to crackers.

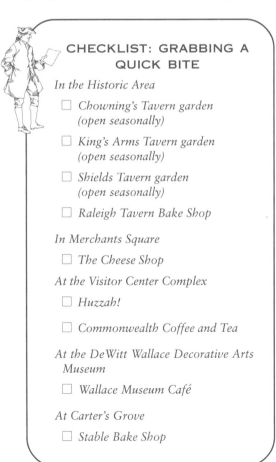

CHECKLIST: GRABBING A QUICK BITE

In the Historic Area

☐ *Chowning's Tavern garden (open seasonally)*

☐ *King's Arms Tavern garden (open seasonally)*

☐ *Shields Tavern garden (open seasonally)*

☐ *Raleigh Tavern Bake Shop*

In Merchants Square

☐ *The Cheese Shop*

At the Visitor Center Complex

☐ *Huzzah!*

☐ *Commonwealth Coffee and Tea*

At the DeWitt Wallace Decorative Arts Museum

☐ *Wallace Museum Café*

At Carter's Grove

☐ *Stable Bake Shop*

DINING IN THE HISTORIC AREA

*Casual dress is appropriate and an admission ticket is
not required to dine in the following establishments*

Chowning's Tavern. When Josiah Chowning opened his tavern in 1766, he promised that "all who please to favour me with their custom may depend on the best of entertainment for themselves, servants, and horses, and good pasturage." That same spirit distinguishes Chowning's Tavern today, although your horses will have to fend for themselves. Mr. Chowning's tavern attracted the ordinary sort, so modern diners will find fare like that served in eighteenth-century British alehouses. Enjoy hearty dishes such as bubble and squeak, Welsh rarebit, Brunswick stew, pulled pork barbecue, black walnut ice cream, and cider cake. A children's menu is available.

Families on the go will find hamburgers and other quick meals in the tavern garden, or you can order from the menu and relax while dining alfresco. (The garden is open seasonally.)

Experience eighteenth-century nightlife at Gambols, offered each evening at Chowning's Tavern. Play backgammon or the royal game of goose, sing along with the balladeers, and be mystified by the magician. Light food and beverages are served.

Christiana Campbell's Tavern. George Washington was a faithful customer of Christiana Campbell's Tavern. In December 1762, he noted in his diary that "Mrs. Washington & children, myself, Colo. Basset, Mrs. Basset & Betcy Bassett all Eat Oysters at Mrs. Campbells." Today, Christiana Campbell's Tavern serves dishes inspired by those the Father of Our Country would have found during his travels throughout the colonies. Enjoy the friendly, informal setting while you feast on Mrs. Campbell's fried chicken, oyster fritters, crab cakes, Carolina fish muddle, deep-dish vermicelli pie, or filet mignon. A children's menu is available.

The tavern garden is open seasonally.

cessful middling customers. Today, visitors dine on fare inspired by recipes in early eighteenth- and nineteenth-century cookbooks. The menu is changed seasonally to reflect the foodstuffs available from local farms, nearby rivers, and the Chesapeake Bay. Try the Shields sampler, salmagundi salad, barnyard chicken roasted on a spit, corn bread-stuffed quail with wild boar sausage, or syllabub. A children's menu is available.

The tavern garden is open seasonally.

Raleigh Tavern Bakery. The smell of gingerbread baking will make your mouth water. Fortunately, you can assuage your hunger with ham biscuits, Sally Lunn bread, rolls, queen's cake, oatmeal "cakes" (cookies), and—yes—gingerbread. Quench your thirst with cider, King's Arms Tavern Ginger Ale, or Chowning's Tavern Root Beer. Enjoy a quick bite from the Bakery as you relax on a bench in the Historic Area.

Mr. Shields welcomes diners to a meal in the tavern garden.

King's Arms Tavern. After Jane Vobe opened the King's Arm Tavern in 1772, it became one of the town's most "genteel" establishments. George Washington sometimes ate here, as did Virginia's future governor Thomas Nelson, Jr. General Baron von Steuben ran up a bill of nearly three hundred Spanish dollars for lodging, meals, and beverages. Present-day diners can savor traditional southern fare such as peanut soup, oyster-stuffed filet mignon, game pie, cavalier's lamb, roast prime rib of beef, and pecan pie. A children's menu is available.

Lunch, beverages, and light fare are served in the garden. (The garden is open seasonally.)

Shields Tavern. In the early 1740s, James Shields took over the tavern that his father-in-law had operated several decades earlier. Shields Tavern attracted lower gentry and suc-

COLONIAL WILLIAMSBURG RESTAURANTS OUTSIDE THE HISTORIC AREA

Unless noted otherwise, casual dress is appropriate and an admission ticket is not required to dine in the following establishments

Carter's Grove Stable Bake Shop. Gaze on the James River while you nibble on ham sandwiches or cookies and sip a soft drink. (An admission ticket is required for entrance to the Carter's Grove grounds and the Stable Bake Shop.)

Huzzah! Contemporary families will likely cheer this fun, casual eatery conveniently located adjacent to the Woodlands Hotel & Suites. Featuring everyday favorites with colonial flair, guests can savor homemade soups, oversized burgers, salads, sandwiches, wraps, pizza, pasta, and cast-iron skillet specialties. Top off any meal with one of Huzzah!'s mouth-watering signature desserts. A children's menu is available for little patriots.

Golden Horseshoe Gold Course Club-

house, Golden Horseshoe Green Course Clubhouse. Each of Colonial Williamsburg's championship golf courses features a clubhouse where you can enjoy both a tasty meal and a picturesque view. Choose from a delightful array of sandwiches, salads, light entrées, and desserts. The "Tidewater's Best" hamburger and "Hole in One" dessert are highly recommended. Both Clubhouses have lounges that serve cocktails and other beverages.

Wallace Museum Café. Stop by the Wallace Museum Café while you are visiting the DeWitt Wallace Decorative Arts Museum. The self-service café offers sandwiches, seasonal salads, soup, chili, and other luncheon fare, tea, and light refreshments, including freshly baked Colonial Williamsburg desserts.

Williamsburg Inn Regency Room. Savor distinctive food and wines in an atmosphere of graceful elegance in the renowned Regency

Room. Enjoy new American cuisine and complement your meal with the perfect wine from our wine list, named an Award of Excellence Winner by *The Wine Spectator* magazine. Breakfast, afternoon tea, and dinner are served daily. Lunch is served Monday-Saturday. Sunday brunch offers a wonderful appetizer and dessert display, scrumptious entrees carefully prepared in the kitchen, champagne, and live music—a very special occasion. Live music also accompanies dinner every evening and dancing is offered Friday and Saturday nights. (Coat and tie are required for dinner and Sunday brunch in the Regency Room.)

Williamsburg Inn Restoration Bar. Enjoy cocktails and conversation at the Williamsburg Inn's newest addition, the Restoration Bar. Commemorating the restoration of Colonial Williamsburg and the creation of the Williamsburg Inn, this clubby setting is ideal for predining gatherings and nightcaps.

Williamsburg Inn Terrace Room. Serving an exquisite selection of tea, this is the perfect gathering spot for traditional afternoon tea. A tempting selection of finger sandwiches, miniature pastries, tartlets, scones, English tea cakes, and cookies are a sampling of tea accompaniments. A light fare menu is also available.

Elegance, superior service, and outstanding food and wines are the hallmarks of the Williamsburg Inn's Regency Room.

Williamsburg Lodge Bay Room. The creative cuisine at the Lodge Bay Room includes regional seafood, grilled steaks, and pasta. Strolling balladeers provide dinnertime entertainment. Breakfast, lunch, and dinner are served daily. At lunch, choose from the menu or the popular soup and salad bar. On the weekend, try the Chesapeake Bay Feast, which features fresh local seafood. Sunday brunch will add the perfect touch to your day of rest. End your meal with a dessert prepared by Colonial Williamsburg's own pastry chefs. A children's menu is available.

Williamsburg Lodge Café. Choose from lighter selections such as soups, salads, sandwiches, and pasta, or dig into grilled steaks, chops, or chicken. Dine to the accompaniment of music from our strolling balladeers. A children's menu is available.

Williamsburg Lodge Garden Lounge. The Garden Lounge features a full selection of beverages, including domestic and imported beers and wines by the bottle or glass.

CHECKLIST: DINING MADE EASY

Colonial Williamsburg restaurants accept the following forms of payment:

- ☐ *Cash*
- ☐ *Traveler's checks*
- ☐ *Colonial Currency**
- ☐ *American Express**
- ☐ *Diners Club**
- ☐ *Discover**
- ☐ *MasterCard**
- ☐ *Visa**

*Merchants Square restaurants do not accept Colonial Currency, and the credit cards accepted by each Merchants Square restaurant vary. Ask your server or the cashier for more information.

DINING IN MERCHANTS SQUARE

Located adjacent to the Historic Area, Merchants Square offers a range of dining experiences. Whether you want a quick bite or a four-course meal, the restaurants and specialty shops here will meet your needs. Grab a sandwich at the **Cheese Shop.** Enjoy lunch or dinner—indoors or out—at **Berret's Seafood Restaurant and Raw Bar, Seasons Café,** or the **Trellis Restaurant and Café.** Top off your meal with **Baskin-Robbins** 31 ice creams or frozen yogurts, sweets from the **Henry Street Chocolatier** or **Wythe Candies & Gourmet Shop,** or peanuts from the **Peanut Shop.**

SHOPPING

George Washington bought earrings at the Golden Ball. Thomas Jefferson purchased books from the Printing Office. Now you can follow in their footsteps.

Ten shops and two outdoor sites in the Historic Area re-create the world of the colonial consumer. You'll see cocked hats, block-printed stationery, sealing wax, jewelry, leather and iron goods, baskets, soaps, candles, Virginia hams, ceramics, and toys. Don't despair if you need modern conveniences such as film and disposable cameras. Just ask—they're stored discreetly under counters and behind curtains, and can be found at Tickets, Treasures and Books (near the Capitol).

Outside the Historic Area, Colonial Williamsburg stores carry a wide range of products for all pocketbooks and all ages, from toys at the Visitor Center shops to fine furniture and home accessories at the Craft House at the Williamsburg Inn. Immediately adjacent to the Historic Area is Merchants Square, a quaint district of fine restaurants and more than forty stores.

For your convenience, purchases from any Colonial Williamsburg store can be delivered to your room at one of our hotels or to the Visitor Center. In addition to cash, Colonial Williamsburg stores accept traveler's checks, and American Express, Diners Club, Discover, MasterCard, and Visa credit cards.

Once you get home, you can order merchandise from Colonial Williamsburg by calling 1-800-770-5938. Shoppers with access to the Internet can view a selection of Colonial Williamsburg products on our Web site at http://www.williamsburgmarketplace.com

SHOPPING IN THE HISTORIC AREA

An admission ticket is not required to visit Historic Area stores

The James Craig Jewelers/Golden Ball Shop. Visitors to the Golden Ball will find many of the same jewelry pieces advertised by James Craig in the eighteenth century. Items such as reproduction stone rings, earrings, pendants, and charms in sterling and fourteen-karat gold are offered for sale along with the magnificent, handcrafted sterling hollowware pieces made next door at the Silversmith shop. Both hand cut and machine engraving is available on-site.

The John Greenhow Store. Visitors to the John Greenhow Store are amazed at the number of items listed on the eighteenth-century broadside advertisement that are for sale in the store today. Advertised "characters" such as Mr. Greenhow, himself, are often on hand in the store to entertain and enlighten the guests to the ways of eighteenth-century mercantilism.

The Mary Dickinson Shop. Step back in time at the Mary Dickinson Shop. Handmade petticoats, short gowns, cloaks, mitts, caps, and beautifully decorated straw hats are all available for purchase. Girls and their mothers will enjoy finding eighteenth-century costumes and hats to enable them to dress up in period-correct style. A large assortment of jewelry, creamware, pewter hollowware, and toiletries reflect eighteenth-century fashion in the best of taste.

McKenzie's Store. Today's visitor to McKenzie's Store will enjoy sampling the candies, and smelling the coffee, tea, and spices, among hundreds of other items for sale in the shop.

The M. Dubois Grocer's Shop. Operating a grocer's shop on this site in the 1770s, M. Dubois advertised delicacies such as chocolate, sugar, raisins of the sun, currants, port wine, French brandy, and Seville oranges. Today, it is the perfect place to find a favorite food gift, such as Virginia hams or preserves. The M. Dubois Grocer is full of delicious smells and delectable treats for our guests of all ages.

The Colonial Post Office. By the middle of 1739, the postal service in the colonies extended from Boston, Massachusetts, through principal towns in New York, Pennsylvania, Maryland, Virginia, North Carolina, and into Charleston, South Carolina. The Colonial Post Office features a large selection of color prints and reproduction printed material. Many of the forms and other printed materials are hand-set and printed below stairs on an eighteenth-century press. Leather-bound books, stationery, quill pens, ink, inkwells, and sealing wax are available. Visitors can buy stamps as well as mail their letters and post cards, complete with a hand-cancelled Williamsburg postmark.

Prentis Store. The building stands today as the best-surviving example of a colonial period store. In continuous use as everything from an apothecary shop to an early twentieth-century gas station, the shell of the store has changed little in its 260-year history. Today, visitors to this fascinating store will see beautifully handcrafted leather goods, eighteenth-century men's clothing and hats, as well as iron hardware and reproduction pottery.

The Raleigh Tavern Bakery. Cookies, cakes, and bread made fresh daily from eighteenth-century recipes. Also, apple cider, root beer, and food-related gifts.

Tickets, Treasures and Books. Tickets, Treasures and Books is a small store offering many historical and nonhistorical publications, games, guest service items, such as cameras and film, as well as operating a ticket office offering admission tickets to all the buildings, carriage rides, and evening programs. The staff of the shop is willing and able to direct guests and answer questions regarding their visit to the historic sites, availability of tickets for special programs, and make dining reservations.

The Tarpley's Store. As a young man, James Tarpley was apprenticed to a merchant to learn his trade and began his own store here in 1755. Not always operated as a "store," Tarpley's served as a place of business for a jeweler, clock maker, and a printer. Much of the merchandise found in Tarpley's store today is geared toward children. Many colorful toys, games, candies, period clothing, and hats, as well as jewelry are available in the store.

OPEN SEASONALLY IN THE HISTORIC AREA

The Colonial Garden and Nursery. The Colonial Garden and Nursery offers a wide variety of heirloom seeds and plants cultivated on-site for sale to our guests. Along with herbs, flowers, seasonal greens, and wreaths, our visitors may purchase appropriate eighteenth-century clay flowerpots,

---

CHECKLIST: SHOPPING MADE EASY

Colonial Williamsburg stores accept the following forms of payment:

☐ *Cash* ☐ *Discover*

☐ *Traveler's checks* ☐ *MasterCard*

☐ *American Express* ☐ *Visa*

☐ *Diners Club*

For your convenience, purchases from any Colonial Williamsburg store can be delivered to your Colonial Williamsburg hotel or to the Visitor Center.

Call 1-800-770-5938 to order Colonial Williamsburg merchandise from home. You can also visit the Colonial Williamsburg catalog at http://www.williamsburgmarketplace.com

---

bird bottles, watering cans, and handcrafted wheelbarrows. Children will enjoy learning about eighteenth-century gardening as they help our trained garden historians and staff cultivate and water the plants in the eighteenth-century garden.

Market Square. Market Square is an open-air market area, with booths resembling those of the eighteenth century, selling baked goods and refreshments, as well as toys, hats, pottery, and baskets. Auctions of new goods from the historic area stores are regularly scheduled weekly throughout the year. Young ladies and gentlemen are encouraged to "dress up" in the eighteenth-century costumes available to rent and experience a taste of eighteenth-century childhood trying their skills at the hoop and stick or bilbo catcher.

COLONIAL WILLIAMSBURG STORES OUTSIDE THE HISTORIC AREA

The Plantation Shop at Carter's Grove. Even if you don't take the tour, stop by for fabulous gifts and souvenirs, many inspired by Carter Grove's early days.

Craft House at Merchants Square. Visitors call this "the most important stop" of all our shops. Something for everyone awaits you on these two levels that highlight reproduction decorative accessories, tabletop, bedding, and collectibles.

Craft House at The Williamsburg Inn. This is the flagship store of Colonial Williamsburg. Featuring reproduction products including eighteenth-century furniture, tabletop, and decorative accessories. The Garden Shop (attached to the main store) is a must-see for enthusiasts. For expert advice on decorating your home Williamsburg style, stop upstairs and visit the Design Studio, a full-service interior design facility.

WILLIAMSBURG Pure Simple Today. One of the newest Foundation-owned shops. One-stop shopping for today's lifestyles. Fill one space or an entire room with twenty-first-century products inspired by Colonial Williamsburg.

Everything Williamsburg! Any other souvenir shop pales in comparison. Apparel, for kids and grownups, plus great kitchen and gift items.

The Gold Course Pro Shop at The Golden Horseshoe Golf Club. Celebrating 37 years, this recently renovated space offers the golfer and style-conscious buyer a wide selection of the top golf brand apparel for ladies and men, plus Golden Horseshoe logo merchandise. (Great gift ideas for the avid golfer from one of the top 100 golf courses in the country.)

The Green Shop at The Golden Horseshoe Golf Club. This shop, which overlooks the eighteenth hole, offers the golfer those must-have items such as towels, golf balls, golf gloves, and accessories. A large selection of ladies' and men's logo apparel make this a must stop for the fashion-conscious golfer.

The Carriage Shop at Governors Inn. Not just sundries. This shop is a microcosm of all the largest Colonial Williamsburg shops: gifts, souvenirs, tavern wares, and, yes, that sunblock.

Williamsburg Booksellers. Books, videos, CDs, and audiotapes relating to the American Revolution, plus many other publications and stationery.

Commonwealth Coffee and Tea. Gourmet coffees and teas, lattés, cappuccino, soft drinks, and delectable pastries.

Williamsburg Marketplace. Gifts, decorative accessories, games, toys, authentic Colonial Williamsburg apparel, and costume rentals.

The Abby Aldrich Rockefeller Folk Art Museum Gift Shop. Mirroring the Colonial Williamsburg museum exhibitions, this shop specializes in American folk art décor and books.

The Regency Shop at The Williamsburg Inn. Looking for a special gift? This is the place. Specially chosen wedding, anniversary, and baby items, all reflective of Colonial Williamsburg style.

The Tidewater Shop at The Williamsburg Lodge. Long renowned for its gardens, this Colonial Williamsburg shop highlights garden-inspired gifts, seasonal gifts, and decorative accessories, plus basic sundries and souvenirs.

The DeWitt Wallace Decorative Arts Museum Gift Shop. Surprise! This is the best-kept secret of all the Colonial Williamsburg shops. Tell the person at the desk that you're "just shopping" and venture downstairs to gifts and accessories reflecting current museum and institute programs.

THE WILLIAMSBURG PRODUCTS PROGRAM

In the 1930s, the Colonial Williamsburg Foundation instituted its landmark Williamsburg Products program by authorizing appropriate manufacturers to produce authentic reproductions based on items within the Foundation collections, or from finds recovered by archaeological expeditions, or found during the original restoration of Colonial Williamsburg.

Subsequently, the Products Program has grown dramatically: there are now more than fifty-two licensees who distribute hundreds of Williamsburg products nationwide, through fine department and specialty stores.

In addition, the Products division produces the Williamsburg Catalog, which is circulated to more than ten million consumers each year. The catalog is also responsible for an interactive e-commerce site, Williamsburg Marketplace, which was launched on July 4, 2000.

The Products Group also operates twenty-eight stores within and adjacent to the Historic Area. The newest of the Colonial Williamsburg owned- and operated-stores is the eighty-five-hundred-square-foot space within the newly expanded Visitor Center, which opened in July 2001. The new store space is roughly divided into two halves: Williamsburg Booksellers and Williamsburg Marketplace. The Booksellers side of the space offers books, magazines, audio-visual products, and other productions for sale to the public, with a smaller space devoted to the Learning Resource Center, for visiting teaching professionals. The Commonwealth Coffee and Tea café offers coffee and other refreshments and light snacks to the visitors. Opposite this space, the Williamsburg Marketplace offers a variety of mementos, keepsakes, and remembrances for the visitor, including gifts, collectibles, and logo apparel.

The stores and catalog offer licensed and proprietary products.

LODGING AND RECREATION

*F*or convenience, old-fashioned hospitality, and things to do, you can't beat Colonial Williamsburg's hotels, ranging from the luxurious Williamsburg Inn to the moderately priced Governor's Inn. Each offers an experience you can't find anywhere else and economical package plans that make it easy to stay with us.

Convenience. Located near the Historic Area—or, in the case of the Colonial Houses, *in* the Historic Area—our Colonial Williamsburg hotels are just steps away from the programs and activities in the restored eighteenth-century capital. You'll also be close to our colonial dining taverns and contemporary restaurants as well as our eighteenth- and twenty-first-century stores. Leave your car at your hotel and walk to the Historic Area. Charge everything from meals to bike rentals to your room. Have your purchases from Colonial Williamsburg's stores delivered to your room for free.

Recreation and Activities. As a guest of Colonial Willliamsburg's hotels, you'll find complete resort facilities and activities. Sports enthusiasts will have plenty to do, from swimming and nature walks to working out and enjoying a massage at the Tazewell Club Fitness Center. Guests of any Colonial Williamsburg hotel can make priority reservations for tee times at the Golden Horseshoe Golf Courses. Our hotels also offer special themed programs throughout the year, such as weekends devoted to gourmet cooking, wine tastings, or a behind-the-scenes look at Colonial Williamsburg.

Package plans. Our package plans offer value and convenience. Many package plans include admission tickets to Historic Area sites, programs, and attractions. Some plans

CHECKLIST: THE ADVANTAGES OF STAYING IN A COLONIAL WILLIAMSBURG HOTEL

☐ *Proximity to the Historic Area and Merchants Square*

☐ *Five hotels to meet everyone's needs, including the only accommodations in the heart of the Historic Area*

☐ *Convenient package plans tailored to a variety of interests and to visiting at different times of the year*

☐ *Preferred reservations at our restaurants, including the colonial dining taverns*

☐ *Special rates at the renowned Golden Horseshoe Golf Courses*

☐ *Discounts on Colonial Williamsburg annual passes*

☐ *Knowledgeable guest services staff to help you purchase admission tickets and plan your day*

☐ *Historic Area-related programs*

☐ *Legendary southern hospitality*

☐ *One-stop billing—charge your meals at our restaurants and purchases at our stores to your room*

☐ *Complimentary delivery of purchases from our stores to your room*

☐ *Use of recreational facilities, including pools, tennis courts, and the Tazewell Club Fitness Center (nominal fee may be required)*

☐ *Children's programs (available seasonally; nominal fee may be required)*

☐ *Complete meeting facilities—hold reunions and other special occasions in a special place*

Call 1-800-HISTORY to make your lodging and dining reservations, purchase admission and evening program tickets, and reserve your tee times. You can also make your reservations and purchase admission tickets on-line at http://www.colonialwilliamsburg.com

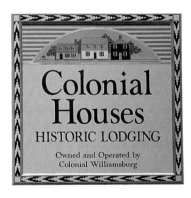

offer special tickets, tours, gifts, or meals. There are packages tailored to special interests, such as golf, and to seasonal events, such as Christmas.

For copies of the Colonial Williamsburg Vacation Planner, annual calendar of events, and current package plan brochure, please call 1-800-HISTORY. You can also make your lodging and dining reservations, purchase admission and evening program tickets, and reserve tee times by calling 1-800-HISTORY. On the Internet, you can find information about our Colonial Williamsburg Hotels at our Web site, http://www.colonialwilliamsburg.com.

Conference and Meeting Facilities. You'll stage an unforgettable meeting at Colonial Williamsburg. Let Thomas Jefferson or Patrick Henry inspire participants, or have fifers and drummers escort attendees to a banquet. For information on how Colonial Williamsburg can revolutionize your next meeting or conference, call 1-800-822-9127, or see our Web site at http://www.colonialwilliamsburg.com.

COLONIAL WILLIAMSBURG HOTELS

Williamsburg Inn. Abby and John D. Rockefeller, Jr., were involved in every aspect of the design, construction, and furnishing of the Williamsburg Inn. They created one of the finest luxury hotels in North America. When the famed philanthropist first built the Inn in 1937, he insisted that "the most possible has been made of each room as regards comfort, convenience and charm." In 2001, Colonial Williamsburg continued to fulfill Rockefeller's original vision through the most extensive interior renovation in the Inn's history spanning the landmark's public spaces and guest rooms, reducing the number from 100 to 62. The refurbishment dually addressed the contemporary needs of twenty-first-century travelers with enhanced services and amenities completing the meticulous restoration.

Just steps from the Historic Area, this elegantly appointed, warm, inviting, classic Virginia resort is now a national historical landmark. Guests have always regarded the Williamsburg Inn as their "second home." The Inn's architecture and ambience reflect those of fashionable nineteenth-cen-

tury spas, where fine dining and a tradition of exceptional hospitality were hallmarks. Employees pride themselves on the kind and courteous service they give every guest, from heads of state to vacationing families.

The Williamsburg Inn has welcomed hundreds of VIPs, including Queen Elizabeth and Prince Philip, the Emperor and Empress of Japan, President and Mrs. Jiang Zemin of China, and countless American presidents. The 1983 Summit of the Industrialized nations, hosted by President Ronald Reagan, and the 1995 NATO and Defense Ministers of America Conferences met at the Williamsburg Inn.

Guests staying in the main building stay in large, spacious rooms furnished with accurate reproductions and antiques of the English Regency style of the early nineteenth century. Providence Hall, nestled on the Inn grounds, affords guests accommodations in a garden setting. From the lobby to the guest rooms, the Inn exudes the quiet luxury of a Virginia country estate. Terraces overlooking the tranquil green countryside invite guests to pause for a moment of relaxation and reflection.

The newly refreshed Regency Room offers distinctive food and wines in an atmosphere of gracious elegance. Music accompanies evening dining and Sunday brunch (coat and tie are required for dinner and Sunday brunch). Commemorating the Inn's renovation is the addition of the Restoration Bar, a comfortably sophisticated spot perfect for enjoying cocktails and conversation before dining or as a nightcap. Superb in-room, private dining provides a casual alternative and a traditional English afternoon tea is always available in the new Terrace Room.

Inn guests can engage in a variety of outdoor activities. The award-winning Golden Horseshoe Golf Courses embrace the south side of the Inn. Just outside the door are swimming pools, tennis courts (both clay and hard surfaces are available), lawn bowling, croquet, nature trails and jogging routes. Guests also enjoy complimentary use of the Tazewell Club Fitness Center.

Children under the age of fifteen can play the 9-hole executive-length Spotswood Course for free when they are accompanied by a paying adult. The Tazewell Club Fitness Center offers summer programs for Inn guests ages five to twelve.

Williamsburg Lodge. The traditions of patriotism and gracious southern hospitality are yours as a guest of the Williamsburg Lodge, located next to the Historic Area. Memories created here last a lifetime.

Relax in a ladder-backed rocking chair on a veranda overlooking a garden. Enjoy quiet conversation, a good book, or a pleasant daydream, or watch a mother duck lead a flotilla of ducklings to the courtyard fountain. Ward off winter's chill by claiming an armchair beside the fireplace in the Lodge's cypress-paneled lobby. Watch as flames from the wood-burning fire cast highlights on handcrafted folk art paintings and carvings inspired by the collection across the street at the Abby Aldrich Rockefeller Folk Art Museum.

Guest rooms feature reproductions from the Abby Aldrich Rockefeller Folk Art Museum. Some rooms have private terraces and balconies overlooking landscaped lawns and gardens. In every season, you will find yourself relaxed, invigorated, and charmed by the surroundings and the hospitality of the Williamsburg Lodge.

The Bay Room offers all-you-can-eat buffets and a wonderful Sunday brunch. Enjoy lighter fare at the Lodge Café and cocktails and conversation in the Garden Lounge.

The Golden Horseshoe Golf Courses, tennis courts (both clay and hard surfaces are available), lawn bowling, croquet, and outdoor swimming pools are literally steps away from the Lodge. Guests also are entitled to complimentary use of the Tazewell Club Fitness Center, which is located right in the Lodge. Nature trails and jogging routes are nearby.

Children under the age of fifteen can play the 9-hole executive-length Spotswood Course for free when they are accompanied by a paying adult. The Tazewell offers summer programs for Lodge guests ages five to twelve.

From large conferences to small retreats, the Williamsburg Lodge Conference Center is the place for your gathering. Conference Center facilities can accommodate up to 700 people at a formal dinner or 850 for a general session. You'll find the perfect blend of inspiration, rest, and opportunity for reflection and recreation at the Lodge Conference Center.

Woodlands Hotel & Suites. Colonial Williamsburg's newest family resort, the Woodlands Hotel & Suites, is located in the Visitor Center complex. Combining the revolutionary experience of eighteenth-century history with the comfort and style of twenty-first-century hotel accommodations, the contemporary, three-story hotel offers guests the highest quality in moderately priced accommodations.

Featuring wood tones, vaulted ceilings, and expansive windows bathing the lobby in natural sunlight, guests of the new Woodlands Hotel & Suites find a natural and comfortable

environment. An oversized fireplace commands the lobby near the dining area for the daily continental breakfast (included in the room rate). The hotel has 204 guest rooms and 96 suites (with a minirefrigerator, microwave, and coffeemaker).

Dining options are sure to please in the Woodlands complex. The new restaurant, Huzzah!, features contemporary favorites with colonial charm all in a family-friendly atmosphere. Guests looking for a quick beverage or tea-time snack will find a tempting selection at Commonwealth Coffee and Tea at the Visitor Center.

Families, couples and business guests find the Woodlands an inviting setting to retire to after a day of sightseeing or meetings. Conference guests find it a quick stroll from the adjacent Woodlands Conference Center catering to groups of all sizes and needs. Refreshing pools, walking trails, miniature golf, and various other recreational activities are right outside the doors. Guests also enjoy priority reservations for tee times at the esteemed Golden Horseshoe Golf Courses. For a nominal fee, guests can work out at the Tazewell Club Fitness Center.

Governor's Inn. Located a short walk from the Historic Area and convenient to the Visitor Center, the Governor's Inn is ideal for those looking for Colonial Williamsburg quality at economical prices. The Governor's Inn caters to families, singles, couples, and seniors who appreciate the value and convenience it offers.

The modern amenities of the spacious, comfortable guest rooms are enhanced by old-fashioned hospitality and service. Take a short walk to the Historic Area, casual and fine dining, and shopping.

Enjoy the sparkling swimming pool located at the Governor's Inn plus use of recreational facilities at the Woodlands. Work out at the

Tazewell Club Fitness Center for a nominal fee. Enjoy special rates at the award-winning Golden Horseshoe Golf Courses.

Colonial Houses. Located in the heart of the Historic Area, the Colonial Houses combine unique eighteenth-century accommodations with twenty-first-century resort activities, restaurants, and shopping. Wake up to the sound of a carriage rolling by your window, then jog on Duke of Gloucester Street or play a round of golf at the Golden Horseshoe. Return to the Revolutionary era with a colonial-style meal at an eighteenth-century tavern. You'll enjoy the best of the past and the present when you stay in one of the Colonial Houses.

The Colonial Houses range in size from larger taverns, such as the Brick House Tavern, to the tiny Lightfoot Laundry tucked away in a garden. Choose a small house for an intimate retreat or a larger one with up to sixteen rooms for a family getaway. Each Colonial House is furnished with period reproductions. Some have canopy beds, working fireplaces, and gardens. Each house also offers the amenities expected by today's vacationer: air conditioning, cable TV with in-room movies, room service, and more.

The Historic Area is outside your door, and the colonial dining taverns, contemporary restaurants, and shopping are just steps away.

All the recreational facilities of the Williamsburg Inn are available to guests of the Colonial Houses. You can also enjoy complimentary use of the Tazewell Club Fitness Center and outdoor pool activities.

Children under the age of fifteen can play the Spotswood Course for free when they are accompanied by a paying adult. The Tazewell Club offers summer programs for five- to twelve-year-old guests of the Colonial Houses.

The Colonial Houses offer unique and memorable lodging for a retreat.

Cascades Motel. Casual atmosphere, moderate prices, and convenient location—just a short walk to the Visitor Center and the Historic Area—make the Cascades Motel another great choice for the entire family.

Surrounded by forty acres of pine forest complete with recreation areas, restful woodlands tones are echoed in the guest rooms, where solid pine and cypress paneling create the backdrop for handcrafted cherry furniture and watercolor scenes. The Cascades Motel has both standard and king-size rooms.

Forest paths wind past a miniture golf course, table tennis areas, horseshoe pits, badminton, shuffleboard, and volleyball courts. Golf equipment may be rented, but there is no other charge for using these facilities.

Huzzah!, a family style restaurant, is well situated on the Visitor Center grounds allowing Cascades Motel guests easy access to enjoyable dining. Guests also enjoy priority reservations for tee times at the revered Golden Horseshoe Golf Courses. For a nominal fee, guests can work out at the Tazewell Club Fitness Center.

RECREATION

The following facilities are available to all guests of Colonial Williamsburg's hotels. Fees may be required for some activities and the use of some facilities. See the previous descriptions for information on the facilities and activities each hotel offers its guests. Information is also available at our Web site, http://www.colonialwilliamsburg.com.

Golden Horseshoe Golf Courses. Located on the grounds of the Williamsburg Inn, the Golden Horseshoe offers some of the finest golf in the country. Golfers can test their skills on two award-winning, 18-hole championship courses or on a 9-hole executive-length course.

Williamsburg's climate makes it possible to play the links here almost year-round. A practice range, rental clubs, electric carts, and golf equipment are available, and a resident professional and his staff offer golf lessons. Golfers wishing to improve their game can also participate in *Golf Digest* Schools. Both the Gold Course and the Green Course Clubhouses feature locker and dressing room facilities, a pro shop, and a full-service restaurant. The Gold Course Clubhouse also has a lounge.

The celebrated Gold Course and Green Course have played hosts to several USGA

THE LEGEND OF THE GOLDEN HORSESHOE

The Legend of the Golden Horseshoe recalls the origins of Virginia History. In 1716, colonial Governor Alexander Spotswood organized a daring expedition to explore the far reaches of the Virginia colony. Spotswood, aware of the frontier's economic potential and bent on encouraging westward settlement, led a party of 63 men on the arduous journey.

Hugh Jones offered his account in 1724 of the toll taken by the rocky soil of the Piedmont and the Blue Ridge: "For this expedition they were obliged to provide a great Quantity of Horse-Shoes (Things seldom used in the lower Parts of the Country, where there are few Stones). The Governor, upon their Return, presented each of his Companions with a Golden Horse-Shoe, some of which I have seen studded with valuable Stones resembling the Heads of Nails."

The recipients became known as the "Knights of the Golden Horseshoe." Although several people in the nineteenth century claimed to have seen them, none of the small, golden horseshoes described by Jones have been found.

The Golden Horseshoe Golf Courses epitomize the tradition and mystique of Spotswood's expedition: the challenge of daring adventure, the enjoyment of a peaceful and spectacular environment, and the reward of completing an arduous test. Colonial Williamsburg invites you to become a modern Knight of the Golden Horseshoe as you test your skills on our three challenging golf courses.

championships. Robert Trent Jones, Sr., called the par 71, 18-hole championship **Gold Course** "my finest" design, describing its location as "a natural arboretum upon which a great golf course has been built." The Gold Course has received numerous honors since it opened in 1963 and *Golf Digest* named it a "Best of the Best Design" recognizing it as one of Jones Sr.'s top six designs. *Golf Magazine* has repeatedly named the classic course one of the "Top 100 You Can Play." *Southern Links* named the par-3 holes the Best of the South. The Gold Course was renovated under the supervision of Robert Trent Jones's son Rees, who is also the architect of the Golden Horseshoe Green Course. Jack Nicklaus holds the course record of a four-under-par 67, a record that has stood since September 19, 1967.

A few months after the **Green Course** opened in 1991, *Golf Digest* selected the par 72, 18-hole championship course as one of the five "Best New Resort Courses." The course features abundant woodland and natural terrain that accommodates various playing skills. Course designer Rees Jones termed it "a shotmaker's course," explaining, "We did not try to make the course tell the player what to do. Instead, we tried to give him several options and allow him to hit several strokes." *Golf for Women* magazine has placed the Green Course among the "Top 100 Women-Friendly Golf Courses."

Robert Trent Jones, Sr., designed the par 31, 9-hole executive-length **Spotswood Course.** Players can hone their short game on this tight, demanding course, which was named the "best 9-hole short course in the country" by *Golf Digest*. Respecting the tradition of the game, players are requested to wear regulation shoes and attire on and around the courses.

Nature and Fitness Trails. Trails are located near the Williamsburg Inn and on the grounds of the Woodlands Hotels & Suites. The Historic Area is also ideal for jogging, power walking, or leisurely strolls.

Tazewell Club Fitness Center. The Tazewell Club Fitness Center at the Williamsburg Lodge offers a full range of fitness services, including sauna, steam room, whirlpool, massage, loofah scrub, aerobics classes, indoor swimming, water aerobics, and Lifecycle, Life-rower, Keiser, Nautilus, and Power Steps equipment.

Conveniently located at the Tazewell Club

Fitness Center, guests can purchase select exercise apparel, accessories, and swim wear at the Tazewell Shop. Bicycle and stroller rentals are available seasonally.

Tennis. Two all-weather and six Har-Tru® clay courts are located adjacent to the Williamsburg Inn Providence Hall. A tennis pro is available for private and semiprivate lessons. The Inn courts also feature a tennis shop where you can rent equipment, purchase tennis clothing and accessories, and register on the guest play list to find a partner. Players are requested to wear regulation tennis shoes and attire on and around the courts.

EDUCATIONAL SERVICES

*A*s part of its mission to preserve and teach America's colonial heritage, the Colonial Williamsburg Foundation offers many educational services.

Learning Resource Center. At the Learning Resource Center, located in the Visitor Center Bookstore, educators, parents, and other interested visitors can talk with Educational Outreach staff about the educational materials, programs, and opportunities for professional development associated with Colonial Williamsburg. The programs and materials here help parents and educators teach colonial American history and prepare children for visits to the Historic Area. Classroom-related materials on eighteenth-century topics, including lesson plans, videos, children's literature, resource kits, and reproduction documents, are available for purchase.

Study Visits. Study Visits provide students —from preschool through college—with an overview of daily life before the American Revolution. Through tours, role playing, and observing and participating in activities, students learn about the lives and choices of the men, women, and children—both free and enslaved—who inhabited the capital city of the largest British colony in North America. Call 1-800-228-8878 for information or to make reservations for Study Visits.

Elderhostel. The Colonial Williamsburg Elderhostel offers educational programs for adults age fifty-five and older. For information, call 757-220-7770.

Electronic Field Trips. Using some of the most advanced technology available for distance learning, Colonial Williamsburg broadcasts live, interactive television programs to students nationwide. Electronic Field Trips bring dramatic presentations directly into the classroom on topics ranging from eighteenth-century methods of fire fighting to slavery to the Stamp Act.

After watching the dramatic portion of the broadcast, students call in to speak with character actors and historians, and listen to questions posed by other children. Registered schools may also access a special site on the Internet where teachers will find related support materials and students can work on educational activities and vote on critical issues raised in the program. For each field trip, registered schools receive a teacher's guide, a poster, primary source materials, and instructions on how to participate. Advance registration and a fee are required to participate in the Electronic Field Trips. Substantial discounts for multiple schools in a school system and schools that choose to view multiple programs are available. Call 1-800-761-8331 for information and to make reservations.

Scouting Programs. Specialized programming for Boy Scouts and Girl Scouts is available. Call 757-565-8737 for more information.

Teacher Institute in Early American History. The Teacher Institute is structured around a series of weeklong programs that provide an in-depth examination of colonial American history as well as an introduction to the interactive teaching techniques in use at Colonial Williamsburg. Designed for elementary and middle school social studies teachers of United States history, these workshops involve participants in early American history "on location." Teachers are immersed in an atmosphere in which they can exchange ideas with historians, meet character interpreters, and take part in reenactments of eighteenth-century events. They study various interactive teaching techniques and create new instructional materials to use in their own classrooms. Visit our Web site at http://www.history.org/teach or call 757-565-8417 for more information.

Colonial Williamsburg Web Site. Visit our Web site, http://www.colonialwilliamsburg.org (or www.history.org), to find a wealth of information about eighteenth-century Williamsburg, the people who lived here, and the places they inhabited. The site also contains material especially for educators, including an overview of educational resources at Colonial Williamsburg and information on Electronic Field Trips for the current school year.

John D. Rockefeller, Jr. Library. Just a few blocks from the Historic Area, the John D. Rockefeller, Jr. Library contains all of Colonial Williamsburg's information resources on the history and culture (including archaeology, architecture, decorative arts, and technology) of the eighteenth-century Chesapeake.

Anyone with a serious interest in the study of the eighteenth-century Chesapeake is welcome to use the library. Patrons can find a wealth of information in the general collections, Virginia reference materials, rare books, manuscripts, maps, microforms, and architectural and photographic collections. In addition, on-line resources, such as CD-ROMs, databases, and user guides, provide enhanced, up-to-date finding aids for hard-to-research materials.

The past meets the present.

GIFTS AND BEQUESTS

Although admission tickets purchased by visitors provide one major source of funds needed to support the educational and museum programs at Colonial Williamsburg, the Foundation needs and encourages gifts and bequests from all who believe in the special Williamsburg experience. Friends interested in discussing gifts to Colonial Williamsburg are encouraged to write the Vice President of Advancement, Box 1776, The Colonial Williamsburg Foundation, Williamsburg, VA 23187, or e-mail at gifts@cwf.org.

The Board of Trustees expresses its deepest thanks to *all* our donors. Since 1926, Colonial Williamsburg's honor roll of donors has grown from its original benefactors to more than 96,000 a year. Listed below are Colonial Williamsburg's most generous benefactors: individuals, foundations, and corporations who have made gifts and grants of $1 million or more.

John D. Rockefeller, Jr.,* and
    Abby Aldrich Rockefeller*

The Annenberg Foundation
Royce R. and Kathryn M. Baker
Mary Lou and George B. Beitzel
Elizabeth* and Miodrag* Blagojevich
Ann-Lee S. and Charles L. Brown
Pauline* and Samuel* M. Clarke
Community Funds, Inc.
Mrs. Owen L. Coon*
Estate of Frances B. Crandol
Mrs. T. Richard Crocker
DeWitt Wallace Fund for Colonial
    Williamsburg
Pat and Jerry B. Epstein
Gloria F. and Martin I. Gersh
The Grainger Foundation
June S. and Joseph H. Hennage
Institute of Museum and Library
    Services
Letitia and Edward C. Joullian
Gretchen B. and William R. Kimball
Dr. Lowry Kirby*
Kresge Foundation
Ambassador Bill and Jean Lane

Ruth P. and Joseph R. Lasser
Estate of Frances M. McDermott
Estate of Inez R. and C.O. Middlekauf
Annie Moose
Marilyn L. Brown and Douglas N. Morton
National Endowment for the Humanities
Abby and George O'Neill
Pew Charitable Trusts
David Rockefeller
John D. Rockefeller Fund
Rockefeller Brothers Fund
Blanchette* and John* D. Rockefeller III
Martha Baird Rockefeller*
Sealantic Fund Inc.
Jane and Marshall* Steel, Jr.
Marshall Steel, Sr. Foundation
Mr. and Mrs. Harold Tanner
Randall L. and Marianne W. Tobias
Lila* and DeWitt* Wallace
Henry H. and "Jimmy" Weldon
Estate of Gladys M. Whitehead
City of Williamsburg
Bob and Marion Wilson
Winthrop Rockefeller Charitable Trust
Leslie Anne Miller and Richard B. Worley

*Deceased

INDEX

*The chief descriptive entries for buildings, sites, or facilities are indicated by page numbers in **boldface** type. An asterisk (*) indicates that a building is an original eighteenth- or nineteenth-century structure. A ■ indicates that you need an admission ticket to see an attraction.*